ETHNIC
CUISINE

ETHNIC
CUISINE

95 GREAT-TASTING RECIPES FROM AROUND THE WORLD

Lorraine Turner

This is a Parragon Publishing Book
First published in 2006

Parragon Publishing
Queen Street House
4 Queen Street
Bath BA1 1HE, UK

ISBN: 1-40548-030-0

Printed in China

Created and produced by the Bridgewater Book Company Ltd

Notes for the reader
This book uses imperial, metric, or US cup measurements. Follow the same
units of measurement throughout; do not mix imperial and metric. All
spoon measurements are level: teaspoons are assumed to be 5 ml, and
tablespoons are assumed to be 15 ml. Unless otherwise stated, milk is
assumed to be low fat and eggs are medium. Some recipes contain nuts.
If you are allergic to nuts you should avoid using them and any products
containing nuts.

Picture acknowledgments
The publisher would like to thank the following for allowing these copyright
images to be used in this book: The Ivy Press: asparagus 47, 96; avocado
12, 50; beet 32; carrots 120, 201; cinnamon 140, 216; cauliflower 156;
cilantro 81, 94, 116; crab 87; eggs 11, 56, 189; green bell pepper 82, 124;
lemongrass/herbs/spices 14, 75; lobster and shrimp 11, 127; mango 198;
parsley 88, 115, 130; peach 190; potato 10, 180; prunes 186; shallots 54,
122; tomato 168. JupiterImages Corporation: apple 204; celery 70; cheese
12, 18; fruit selection 10; garlic 26, 69, 93, 139, 167, 174; greens 12; herbs
12; leafy vegetables 12; meat 11; mushroom 150, 170; oil bottles 16; onion
48, 104, 118; pecans 219; pomegranate 202.

CONTENTS

INTRODUCTION

This book is a celebration of ethnic cuisine, but what exactly is ethnic food? When we use the term here, we are focusing not so much on the food of a few minority communities, but more on the cuisines of many rich and varied societies and cultures around the world, whether large or small. As a result, Ethnic Cuisine is truly global in its diversity, from mouthwatering Eastern dishes such as Mongolian Firepot, Indonesian Chili Shrimp and Khandvi, to the delicious fare of Europe and the West, such as Irish Fish Pie, Scotch Broth and Sicilian Tuna.

Culinary evolution

International cuisines evolve and change due to a wide range of different conditions, whether economic, climatic, geographic, or political. For example, in Russia, the long, cold winters have created a need for foods that provide energy and warmth; foods very rich in slow-burning carbohydrates and fats, such as rye breads and porridges, hearty beef stews, and cereals and beans.

In Indonesia, where a large group of islands gives rise to many miles of coastline, fish and

shellfish dishes abound. The cuisine of this region has also been influenced by foreign merchants and travelers, who over the centuries have introduced different ingredients to the islands, such as chilies, bell peppers, tomatoes, and peanuts. Mexico also has many miles of coastline, and as a result its cuisine is rich in seafood. But additionally, it is fortunate to have good agricultural land and a warm climate suitable for cultivating tropical plants, so here you will also find beef, pork, and lamb, as well

as cheeses, avocados, chocolate, and a variety of spices and herbs. In Greece, where you are never more than a couple of hours' drive from the sea, a wide selection of fish is always on the menu. Greek cuisine has, however, also been heavily influenced by a series of invasions over the centuries, especially by the Turks. As a result, the food often has an Eastern influence. For example, Baklava, the sumptuous syrup-drenched dessert found all over Greece, is Turkish in origin.

Regional diversity

The larger the country and the more varied the terrain and climate, the more wide-ranging its cuisine tends to be. In Spain, for example, the dishes vary widely between regions, from the hot southern province of Andalucia, where the food is spicy with an Arabic influence, to the cooler northern province of Galicia, where you will find hearty soups and stews, and hints of its Celtic past. In India, the diet has been affected not just by climate and geography, but by religion and caste. So some Indians—for example some Brahmins, are vegetarians, while others nearer the coast eat fish too. And in the huge expanse of North America, the diet has been affected as much by immigrants from

Europe and beyond as it has by climate and terrain. Creole cooking can be largely traced back to French settlers in New Orleans in the 17th century, and the French seafood stew known as Bouillabaisse evolved there in the Deep South into what is now called Gumbo.

A succession of explorers and settlers from different countries influenced the original diet of the West Indian region now known as the Caribbean, where there is an abundance of fresh seafood, meat, vegetables, and tropical fruit. The resulting mixture of dishes and cuisines is remarkably varied. Coconut is widely used—coconut ice cream, for example, is loved for its satisfyingly rich flavor and yet it is refreshingly cool on those hot, balmy days and nights.

Taste the world

The recipes in this book sample the flavors of a huge range of exciting cuisines from around the world, with delicious dishes to suit every occasion. They are simple to make and require no special equipment apart from the basic essentials, so you will find it reassuringly easy to bring wonderfully exotic tastes and aromas from different parts of the globe into your kitchen, wherever you live.

HEALTHY EATING AROUND THE WORLD

Delicious, nutritious food, lovingly prepared, is the mainstay of a healthy life, and each nation around the world has developed its own way of fulfiling this basic need, sometimes in spite of considerable adversity.

Stir-frying and preservation

In China, they have developed a wonderfully versatile style of cooking. The stir-fry is supremely adaptable—it suits all kinds of meat, poultry, fish, and vegetables. Savvy Chinese cooks can assemble a stir-fry from whichever foodstuffs are available at the time, and can replace any ingredients at the drop of a hat. For example, if you have no chicken or turkey readily available, you can simply cut up some protein-rich tofu and use that instead. If you have no Napa cabbage, then cut up and throw in whichever green vegetables are to hand. This ability to mix or replace different ingredients is particularly useful in times of hardship or scarcity. It is said that Chinese peasants know every edible wild plant that grows in their environment. Most of these are not ordinarily used in the kitchen, but in lean times they can be used as acceptable and nutritious substitutes. Stir-frying has the benefit of being a very healthy way to cook, since it requires a minimum amount of fat and only a very short cooking time, which helps to retain all the nutrients.

Preserving surplus food in times of abundance is a way of ensuring an adequate supply in times of hardship, and Chinese cooks are masters of this art too. Their methods of preservation include drying, pickling, smoking, salting, sugaring, and soaking in different soy sauces.

Fresh and raw

The Japanese have also developed their own way of healthy eating. They usually cook foods as lightly as possible. In fact, they eat many fish dishes and sushi raw in order to preserve their nutrients. Cooking food does help to destroy potentially harmful bacteria, however, so when preparing raw foods in dishes, Japanese cooks use only the freshest ingredients.

Hot and spicy

Cooking is not the only way to destroy harmful bacteria. It is no accident that the hotter and wetter a climate is, the spicier the food tends to be. Scientists have observed that nations with hot climates, such as Ethiopia, India, Kenya, Indonesia, Iran, Malaysia, Nigeria, Mexico, Thailand, and Morocco, use spices in almost every dish. Part of the reason why they do this is because certain hot spices have an antibacterial effect—they help to prevent food spoilage and reduce the risk of food poisoning. Some spices also make powerful fungicides.

An armory of aromatics

Spices are often more effective when combined with others than when used on their own. As a result, certain combinations of spices have become popular in different countries. For example, in Chinese cuisine, a well-known combination is Asian five-spice powder, which comprises fennel seeds, cloves, star anise, cinnamon, and Szechuan peppercorns. In India, the combination known as *garam masala* can contain any or all of the following spices: black pepper, cardamom, cinnamon, cloves, coriander seeds, cumin, dried chilies, fennel, mace, and nutmeg, among others. Chili powder is another popular combination in India, but it has also become widely used around the world. It usually contains a mixture of garlic, cumin, onion, coriander seeds, oregano, and dried red chilies. And Tunisians have their own five-spice combination called *gâlat dagga*, used to flavor Arabic stews, which comprises pepper, grains of paradise, cinnamon, cloves, and nutmeg.

But interesting spice combinations are not always confined to hot or tropical countries. In France, for example, the combination known as *quatre épices* (four spices) is a very old favorite and usually comprises any four of the following: cinnamon, cloves, ginger, nutmeg, and white pepper. It probably came into its own in old, pre-Revolutionary France, to help reduce food spoilage before refrigeration methods were invented. Nevertheless, the cooler the climate, the less there is a need for spices—in Finland and Norway, for example, spices are used much less often in dishes.

Going native

The cuisine of each country evolves according to its climate and other factors, but always with an eye to good health. This is one of the reasons why some nutritional experts advise people traveling abroad to eat freshly cooked local cuisine because it is likely to be the healthiest food you will find in that part of the world.

NUTRITION AND HEALTHY FOOD

A well-balanced daily diet is essential for good health and wellbeing and it is equally important to follow sound nutritional principles when eating ethnic foods, either in your home country or when traveling abroad. The most effective way to do this is by including foods from the five main nutrient groups in the correct proportions. These nutrient groups are carbohydrates, proteins, fats, vitamins, and minerals.

Carbohydrates

These are an important energy source for the body. All carbohydrates fall into one of two groups: simple and complex. Simple carbohydrates burn off in the body very quickly. They are found mainly in sweet, sugary foods, such as honey, sugar, cakes, and candies. Although they are a quick source of energy, another top-up will be needed fairly quickly in order to keep going. Therefore, it is better to major on complex carbohydrates, which burn more slowly. Complex carbohydrates have a more complicated structure than simple carbohydrates and they take longer to break down. Whole grain varieties of starchy foods such as bread or rice are especially beneficial.

You can find plenty of carbohydrates in foods wherever you are in the world. For example, potatoes are easy to find all over the globe, from jacket potatoes and French fries in North America and Britain, to Bombay potatoes in India. Bread is also easy to find and is rich in

carbohydrates, whether you choose a delicious *pain rustique* in France or a mouthwatering naan bread in India. You could also opt for rice or noodles in Asia, or pasta in Italy. In Mexico, try one of the many exciting bean dishes wrapped in flour tortillas, or in the Peruvian Andes choose the delicious grain known as quinoa. In the Middle East, you could choose dishes accompanied by bulgar wheat. In Greece and Cyprus you could opt for vegetable dishes accompanied by cracked wheat (known as *pourgouri*). And in North Africa you could choose couscous to accompany one of the many vegetable dishes available there.

Proteins

Proteins are an important building block for the development and growth of the body. Again they fall into one of two types: incomplete and complete. Incomplete proteins can be found in beans, grains, and green leafy vegetables. They provide only some of the amino acids that the body requires, so need to be combined with at least one complete protein food to ensure an adequate intake.

Complete proteins contain all the essential amino acids, and in ethnic dishes you will find them mainly in foods from animal sources, such as meat, poultry, fish, seafood, eggs, and dairy products, and also in soybean products such as soy milk and tofu.

You will find it very easy to choose protein-rich foods wherever you are in the world. Ethnic dishes containing meat or poultry are available almost everywhere. Look for curries made with pork and lamb in India, stir-fries made with beef, pork, and chicken in China, or lamb kabobs in Greece and India and beef steaks, roast chicken, and turkey in North America and Europe. Ethnic dishes containing seafood are equally easy to find, from Spanish seafood paella, to Chinese baked fish and Thai fish curry. If you are vegetarian, choose dishes that contain cheese, eggs, or tofu, and for extra protein accompany them with pulses and grains. You could opt for a cheese fondue or omelet in France or Switzerland, or stir-fried tofu and beans on a bed of egg-fried rice in China.

Fats

Fat is an important nutrient for the body and is a valuable source of energy. However, some fats are better for the body than others. Try to restrict your intake of saturated fats because an excess can cause blocked arteries and raised cholesterol levels. You will find saturated fats in butter and shortening, and the fat in meat and other dairy products.

Monounsaturated fats are better for you, and can be found in plant oils such as olive oil. One of the reasons the Mediterranean diet is so healthy is because it uses healthy olive oil rather than butter. Polyunsaturated fats are also good for you, and you can find them in canola oil, sesame oil, nuts, and seeds, which are popular in Chinese cooking.

Essential fatty acids (EFAs) have been hailed as the best fats of all, because they help to renew and repair cells, regulate heart rate and blood pressure, increase fertility, and promote growth in children. The following ethnic foods are rich in EFAs: olive, canola, and flaxseed oils; oily fish such as salmon, mackerel, sardines, anchovies, and tuna; nuts; seeds; dark-green leafy vegetables, such as spinach, kale, and cabbage.

To eat healthily around the globe, choose dishes cooked in canola, peanut, or sesame oil in Asia, or olive oil in Europe. Eat plenty of oily fish, such as chargrilled tuna steaks in North America and Europe, or mackerel escabeche in Spain. Also opt for nuts and seeds, such as chicken and cashew nuts in China, or hummus made with chickpeas and sesame-seed paste in Greece and Cyprus. And eat dark-green leafy vegetables wherever possible, such as dolmades (stuffed vine leaves) in Greece, or steamed mackerel on a bed of spinach in Asia or Europe.

Vitamins and minerals

Vitamins are essential for good health and vitality, and for fighting off disease. You should try to gain a working knowledge of the main vitamins and minerals to make sure that you are getting an adequate supply of them.

Some vitamins, such as vitamins A and D, dissolve in fat, while others, such as the B group and C, dissolve in water. Vitamin C is easily replenished daily by foods containing fruit or vegetables such as Spanish gazpacho, a French salade Niçoise, or a fresh fruit salad from the USA, while Japanese sushi will provide a good supply of vitamin D.

It is also important for your body to have an adequate supply of minerals, such as calcium, iodine, iron, magnesium, phosphorus, and zinc. The best sources of calcium are dairy products, which are rarely used in Chinese cuisine, but Chinese and Japanese cooks use a lot of tofu, sesame seeds, canola oil, and sesame oil in their cooking, which are also rich in calcium and can help to restore the balance. Eating a wide variety of foods will ensure enough minerals are eaten. Mexican chili beans provide iron in the diet and an Asian fish curry with noodles will supply a source of iodine.

Finally, some vitamins can be toxic if taken in excess. As always, the best method is to ensure that you eat a varied, well-balanced diet, and consult your doctor or a qualified nutritionist if you are in any doubt.

BALANCING YOUR VITAMINS AND MINERALS

It is important to ensure you get a good intake of vitamins and minerals from ethnic foods. Here are some of the most important vitamins and minerals, and worldwide dishes that can help you eat a balanced and healthy diet. The list is not comprehensive, so you may need to do some of your own research.

Vitamin/ Mineral	Source of vitamin or mineral
Vitamin A	Any dishes containing carrots, eggs, dairy products, and green and yellow vegetables. Try stir-fried carrots, corn, and snowpeas in China, or vegetable samosas in India.
Vitamin B1	Try ethnic husks, whole wheat, peanuts, and pork. Most vegetables or milk will supply useful amounts. Look for satay sauce in India, or whole grain rice in many parts of the world.
Vitamin B2	Any dishes containing cheese, fish, eggs, or leafy green vegetables. Look for 'à la Florentine' dishes, fondues, and cheese sauces throughout Europe, and steamed fish dishes in Asia.
Vitamin B6	Look for beef steaks in Europe and the Americas, or stir-fried beef or cabbage dishes in Asia. Look for brewer's yeast, wheatgerm, liver, milk, or eggs.
Vitamin B12	Try Italian Spaghetti Bolognese topped with cheese, or look for stir-fried beef or pork, or sweet-and-sour pork balls in China. Try liver, beef, pork, eggs, milk, or cheese.
Vitamin C	Choose dishes that contain citrus fruits, berries, tomatoes, potatoes, sweet potatoes, or green leafy vegetables. Look for fruit salads, potato, and tomato dishes all over the world.
Vitamin D	Any dishes containing fish liver oils, sardines, salmon, tuna, herring, or dairy products. Look for fish dishes such as gravad lax in Scandinavia, or ceviche in South America.
Vitamin E	Any dishes containing soybeans or tofu in Asia, Europe, and North America, or dishes with green leafy vegetables. Also found in wheatgerm, eggs, cereals, spinach, or greens.
Calcium	Any dishes containing milk, cheese, soybeans, sardines, dried beans, salmon, peanuts, or sesame seeds. Try a feta salad in Greece, Bangladeshi chicken, or vegetable korma made with yogurt.
Iodine	Dishes that contain seafood, onions, or kelp will be rich in iodine. In France, you could choose an onion soup, tart, or bouillabaisse, or a baked fish with a chermoula marinade in Morocco.
Iron	Any dishes containing red meats, kidney, heart, liver, egg yolks, oysters, nuts, beans, asparagus, or oatmeal. Choose chilli con carne in South America, or a beef or pork stir-fry with nuts in China.
Magnesium	Any dishes that contain figs, grapefruit, lemons, nuts, seeds, apples, or dark-green vegetables. Choose fresh figs and Prosciutto in Italy or a pork and apple stir-fry in Asia.
Phosphorus	Any dishes with meat, poultry, fish, whole grains, nuts, seeds, or eggs. Choose roast chicken or turkey, or ham and eggs in North America or Europe, or a fish curry with rice in China.
Zinc	Any dishes containing steak, lamb, pork, wheatgerm, eggs, brewer's yeast, or pumpkin seeds. Choose lamb chops or steaks in North America or Europe, or sweet-and-sour pork in China.

THE ETHNIC PANTRY

A well-stocked pantry is an essential part of a good kitchen, and storing some basic essentials will ensure that you can prepare satisfying ethnic meals for any occasion, and at short notice if necessary.

Herbs

In addition to growing fresh herbs in your garden or in pots on a windowsill, a good stock of dried herbs is essential. You can also store a surplus of some fresh exotic herbs in the freezer—ideal for those occasions when they are unavailable in your local store. Here are some herbs that you will find useful in ethnic cooking. There is no need to buy the dried herbs all at once—simply add them to your pantry when needed.

Basil, Thai basil, holy basil Use fresh. Delicious with tomatoes, potatoes, rice, pasta, garlic, olive oil, and lemon.

Bay leaf Can use fresh, but dried is fine. Ideal in soups, sauces, pickles, stews, and custards.

Cilantro, Vietnamese cilantro (rao ram) Use fresh. Excellent with most savory dishes, particularly hot chili dishes, stir-fries, and dressings.

Dill Use fresh. Mixes well with fish, eggs, potatoes, and other vegetables, rice and beans, and is good in sauces, dressings, and marinades.

Epazote Buy dried. This Mexican herb combines well with pork and fish, and is excellent in chili and bean dishes.

Fennel Use fresh. Partners well with fish, potatoes, rice, and beans.

Flat-leaf parsley Use fresh. A versatile herb that is used widely in savory dishes, salads, stuffings, and butters.

Garlic, chives, (including Chinese chives) and onion Excellent in a wide range of savory dishes, salads, sauces, stuffings, and dressings.

Kaffir lime leaves Can buy fresh, but dried is fine. Used widely in Thai and Indonesian dishes, including soups, stir-fries, stews, and curries.

Lemongrass Buy fresh stalks, although can be

bought dried. Goes well with meat, poultry, fish, and vegetables, and is used widely in Thai cuisine. Excellent in soups, stir-fries, dressings, and marinades.

Marjoram and oregano Use fresh or dried. Delicious with poultry, fish, eggs, cheese, tomatoes, and beans. They lend their flavor well to sauces, stews, pizzas, and marinades.

Mint Use fresh. Pairs particularly well with lamb, potatoes, peas, and yogurt, and is delicious in soups, salads, meat, and vegetable dishes, sauces, dressings, desserts, and drinks.

Mitsuba Buy fresh. This Japanese parsley is ideal with fish and vegetables, and is used to flavor soups and sauces.

Myrtle Use fresh. Combines well with meat, game, and fish, and is good in marinades. It is particularly popular in Sicilian cooking.

Rosemary Use fresh or dried. An ideal partner for lamb, oily fish, potatoes, beans, garlic, and wine, and delicious in marinades.

Sage Best to use fresh, but can buy dried. Excellent with meat, fish, and eggs, and ideal in sauces and stuffings.

Sansho This dried and ground Japanese herb is ideal with fish and tofu, and good in soups and dressings.

Tarragon Use fresh. This herb has a very strong flavor and should be used in moderation. It goes particularly well with poultry and eggs, and imparts an excellent flavor to vegetable dishes, salads, and sauces.

Thyme Use fresh or dried. Mixes particularly well with eggs, nuts, red wine, mushrooms, and tomatoes, and is excellent in soups, stews, sauces, pâtés, and marinades.

Spices

You can never have enough spices in ethnic cuisine. In addition to the spice combinations mentioned previously, here are a few of the main spices that you will find handy:

Cardamom, green Available as whole pods or as ground seeds from the pods. Used in curries and pastries, and to flavor drinks.

Chili powder This blend of ground spices comes with varying degrees of heat, and is used to add a fiery kick to a wide variety of savory meat, poultry, and vegetable dishes.

Cinnamon Available as whole sticks or ground. Excellent in a variety of cakes, desserts, and drinks.

Cloves Available whole or ground. Particularly good with ham and apples, and in desserts.

Coriander Available as seeds or ground. Used to flavor meat and poultry dishes, and also good with vegetables.

Cumin Available as seeds or ground. Excellent in poultry dishes and with vegetables.

Ginger The fresh root has a lemon flavor, but takes on a sweeter flavor when dried and ground. It is used widely in Asian cooking, particularly in stir-fries, chutneys, cakes, and desserts.

Mustard seeds (black) Used in Indian savory dishes to add pungency.

Nutmeg Best freshly grated from a whole nutmeg, but also available ground. Widely used in savory dishes, sauces, and desserts.

Paprika Lends a spicy flavor and red color to a variety of savory dishes and sauces. Smoked paprika is particularly aromatic.

Peppercorns Extremely versatile with a wide range of uses in savory dishes, and some desserts.

Saffron Available as dried threads or ground. Expensive, but imparts a lovely flavor and yellow color to dishes, especially paellas and risottos.

Turmeric This ground spice is a cheaper alternative to saffron, and is often used in curries.

Noodles and grains

You will find a supply of fresh and dried noodles and grains very useful for quick, easy meals. Chinese egg noodles and rice noodles are ideal for soups, stir-fries, and as an accompaniment to main meals. Different-shaped pastas, including long ribbons or strands and sheets of lasagne, short shapes such as shells, tubes, and quills, and tiny soup pasta, are also excellent staples to keep in store. Long-grain white and brown rices, such as basmati and jasmine, are perfect for many Indian or Asian savory dishes, while medium-grain rice is great for paellas and sushi, and short-grain rice, such as risotto, is ideal for a risotto dish. Finally, keep some couscous and bulgur wheat handy, too—quickly reconstituted with boiling water, they make good, easy accompaniments for savory dishes and salads.

Oils and vinegars

Always keep plenty of good-quality olive oil and extra virgin olive oil on hand. You will find them invaluable for cooking as well as for drizzling over pizzas and salads. Vegetable oil, peanut oil, and sesame oil are ideal for stir-fries, and sunflower seed oil and canola oil are perfect for all types of cooking, including deep-frying (but do not use canola oil for dressings because it has a strong flavor).

Balsamic vinegar lends a deliciously sweet, syrupy taste to salads and, believe it or not, to strawberries. Buy the best you can afford for a superior taste and texture. You will also find it useful to keep some wine vinegars handy, such as red, white, and sherry. Cider vinegar is good with meat and cheese dishes, and rice vinegar is excellent in a wide range of Asian dishes, including soups, sauces, and marinades.

Beans

Dried beans are essential items in any pantry, but time-consuming to prepare and cook, so you should also keep some canned varieties for quick, impromptu meals. You can add them to your pantry gradually, but a good selection to start with would be red kidney beans and lima beans for soups, stews, and sauces; kidney beans and soybeans for soups and curries; fermented black beans, which are very popular in Chinese stir-fries and sauces; chickpeas for dips such as hummus and for soups, salads, and stews; and lentils for soups, sauces, stews, and other savory dishes. However, it is worth keeping dried split lentils in store, for use in dishes such as Indian dhal, since they do not need presoaking or lengthy cooking like dried beans.

Nuts and seeds

Do not buy these in large quantities because they do not store well for long periods. If they are unshelled, keep them in the refrigerator. The following selection will help you get started: almonds for savory dishes and salads, as well as cakes and desserts; pecans, which are very popular in American dishes, such as Mississippi Mud Pie; cashew nuts, which are much loved in Chinese cooking, especially in stir-fries;

pistachios, ideal in stuffings and desserts; pine nuts, which are excellent in salads, rice dishes, pasta sauces, and desserts; sunflower seeds, which are good in granola, salads, and breads; pumpkin seeds, again good in granola and breads; and sesame seeds, which are delicious in stir-fries and some Chinese desserts.

Sauces and condiments

Soy sauce is essential for Asian stir-fries, sauces, and marinades, and hoisin sauce is another popular favorite, along with sweet chili sauce. Chinese plum sauce is good with dishes such as Peking Duck, while Tabasco is excellent for imparting a fiery kick to Mexican salsas. Thai fish sauce and Thai curry paste, both red and green, are widely used in Thai cuisine. A selection of mustards, including Dijon, would be useful and sesame seed paste is essential for some Middle Eastern soups, sauces, and dips. Miso is good for thickening and flavoring Japanese soups, while brown sauce and tomato ketchup are traditional accompaniments for a variety of American and British dishes. Finally, you will find strained canned tomatoes and tomato paste invaluable for making quick, tasty meals where the focus is on tomatoes, such as pasta sauces and pizza toppings.

Canned ingredients

In addition to canned beans, you will find a selection of canned fish useful. Good ones to keep stock of are anchovies, sardines, tuna, salmon, and crabmeat. Also store some canned olives, tomatoes, coconut milk (ideal for Thai and Indonesian dishes), corn, bamboo shoots, and water chestnuts.

Other useful items

You will also find the following items useful: dried fruits and berries, stock cubes, gelatin, vanilla beans or extract, chocolate, honey, unsweetened cocoa, palm sugar or brown sugar, dry unsweetened coconut, and a selection of alcohol, including rice wine, red and white wine, sherry, and cider.

Refrigerator and freezer essentials

Keep a supply of eggs and milk handy, and thick, plain yogurt. Plain yogurt is used around the world, especially in American, Mediterranean, and Indian cooking. Also keep some firm all-purpose cheeses, such as Cheddar and Parmesan, and some good-quality natural cream cheese. For richer recipes, use cream or sour cream. Tofu, both firm and silken, is another worthwhile staple to keep in the refrigerator.

In addition to freezing fresh herbs, you should also keep in your freezer some shrimp, a variety of firm fish fillets, a selection of vegetables, some berries (such as raspberries and cranberries) and perhaps some sherbet, frozen yogurt, and/or ice cream.

Substituting ingredients

For the most successful results, it is always best to stick to the ingredients specified in a recipe, but if an item is unavailable, then with a little care and ingenuity you can experiment with ingredients that have similar qualities or flavors in order to create a suitable alternative. For example, kaffir lime leaves can often be replaced with grated lime rind, and the juice and rind of lemons and limes are often interchangeable. If you do not have coconut milk, 1 cup of coconut milk can be replaced with 3 tablespoons of canned cream of coconut and a generous 3/4 cup of water. If a recipe calls for yogurt but you do not have any to hand, try replacing 1 cup of plain yogurt with 1 cup of whole milk plus 1 tablespoon of lemon juice. Finally, if you cannot find rice wine, try using a similar quantity of sherry instead.

EQUIPMENT, PREPARATION, AND PRESENTATION

You do not need a lot of expensive special equipment to cook delicious international dishes; just a good selection of different-size pans, skillets, mixing bowls, knives, and bakeware. Even a food processor, while convenient, is not essential. It is also unnecessary to buy a pasta machine or other equipment for making pasta shapes and noodles— good-quality fresh pastas and noodles are widely available nowadays, so you do not need to make your own. However, there are some basic items that you will use time and time again, for many different cuisines or dishes, so it is worthwhile choosing and investing in the best.

Cookware essentials

It is well worth having good-quality equipment. Investing in a wok is a good idea for stir-frying. A large pan is very versatile. The pan should be stainless steel with a copper base or with a thick layer of aluminum—which will ensure even cooking and guard against ingredients catching on the base. It should also have a tight-fitting lid, to seal in the ingredients and avoid evaporation. A casserole is another essential item for cooking a variety of dishes, and it must be heavy-duty and ovenproof, so that part of the cooking can be done on the stove before being transferred to the oven. Stainless steel or enameled cast iron are the best options, rather than earthenware. Again, it should have a heavy, tight-fitting lid.

Choosing and seasoning a wok

A wok is extremely useful for cooking stir-fries and a wide range of other Chinese and Thai dishes. It can also be used as an Indian Kadhai as well as a deep-fat fryer.

When buying a wok, choose a large, good quality one, since if a wok is too loaded with food, the food will steam instead of fry. For a successful stir-fry, there must be enough room in the wok for the food to be tossed continually around it, with as much food as possible coming into contact with the hot sides of the pan. For this reason, the larger the wok, the better.

Woks come in different materials, such as stainless steel, cast iron, and carbon steel.

Carbon steel tends to be the most highly recommended, because it heats and cools quickly and is therefore very convenient to use. You can choose a wok with a rounded or flat base, but you will find that a flat-based wok is more practical for use on a conventional stove, as well as being safer. Woks are also available with one or two handles—you can choose whichever you prefer.

When you get your wok home, first wash it in clean, soapy water, then rinse and dry it thoroughly. Now you will need to season it. Heat the wok on the stove until it is hot. While it is heating, soak a wad of clean paper towels in 1–2 tablespoons of vegetable oil, then put it between a pair of heatproof tongs or chopsticks and rub it all over the hot inner surface of the wok. Let the oiled wok heat on the stove for 10 minutes, then remove from the heat. Wipe it clean with some clean paper towels, then repeat the process: heat the wok, oil the hot inner surface with vegetable oil and heat for 10 minutes. Now remove from the heat, wipe clean with paper towels (do not use soap and water) and store until ready to use.

When you use the wok, heat it well before adding any oil. And after you have used it, clean with hot water only, not soap. Use a brush to clean it but not an abrasive surface. Dry it with paper towels and grease lightly with vegetable oil. Eventually, it will develop a wonderful patina, which is the pride of all Asian cooks.

In Chinese and Thai cooking the wok can be used for everything and all types of food—curries, soups, stir-fries, and noodles may be cooked in it. Asian cooks cut ingredients for stir-fries into small, similar-size morsels for quick, even cooking.

Other useful items

Rice steamers or cookers are useful for cooking rice for Chinese or Japanese dishes. A casserole or a large pan may also be used for risottos or paellas, but paella pans are well suited for the task—they have wide sides that are designed to expose a wide surface area so the liquid evaporates before the rice becomes overcooked. A large pan with an even distribution of heat is important as rice trebles in size during cooking, and the rice is less likely to stick or burn. Other specialist ethnic utensils include clay or terracotta casserole dishes used in Spanish and South American cooking. They are left unglazed on the outside so they can absorb heat and moisture, but have a smooth, glazed interior. They are suitable for use in the oven or microwave. Traditional polenta pots made of unlined copper may also be useful. They are narrower at the bottom than at the top allowing the heat to be distributed evenly.

Authentic touches

For authentic ethnic cuisine it is worth considering the culture associated with the food you are serving. Whichever dish you are preparing, pay attention to how the cooks of that country prepare and present it. In Italian cooking, simplicity is the essence so that the flavor of ingredients is not masked by elaborate sauces or served with flamboyant garnishes. Italian fish dishes may be served with just a few herbs, a splash of olive oil, and a wedge of lemon to squeeze over it. In Japan, dishes are not highly seasoned, to allow the flavor of the main ingredients to shine through. Flavors are often added with condiments or dipping sauces, and dishes are always served with rice. In Indian cooking, the cook strives for a mixture of flavors and textures across a number of dishes, which are often presented together, including the dessert. At a Chinese meal, each person is given his or her own bowl of rice while other dishes are served in communal bowls, shared by everyone sitting at the table.

Japanese and Thai cooks are famous for their presentation skills—their dishes are light and elegant, and often attractively decorated with a variety of flourishes, such as scallion tassels. Color is also important—for example, Indian and Spanish cooks often use saffron and turmeric to give a beautiful yellow color to their rice dishes.

Finally, remember that, whereas knives, forks, spoons, plates, and cups with handles are ideal for many Western meals, chopsticks, and serving bowls, porcelain spoons, and small teacups without handles will create the right atmosphere for Asian meals, and in particular those inspired by Chinese and Thai cuisine.

Soups, Appetizers, and Snacks

The tantalizing dishes in this section will whet your appetite and offer a tasty appetizer or light meal.

Turmeric Yogurt Soup

The zingy, vibrant yellow of this creamy vegetarian soup is the unmistakable hue of turmeric, used to color many Indian dishes. Grown on the large spice plantations of southern India, turmeric is used both in the kitchen and as an antiseptic.

SERVES 4–6

PREP TIME 5 MINUTES

COOKING TIME 15 MINUTES

⅓ cup gram flour

1 tsp ground turmeric

¼ tsp chili powder

½ tsp salt

1¾ cups plain yogurt

2 tbsp ghee or 2 tbsp vegetable or peanut oil

3 cups water

to garnish

½ tbsp ghee or ½ tbsp vegetable or peanut oil

¾ tsp cumin seeds

½ tsp black mustard seeds

½ tsp fenugreek seeds

4–6 whole fresh red chilies, depending on how many you are serving

1 Mix the gram flour, turmeric, chili powder, and salt together in a large bowl. Using a whisk or fork, beat in the yogurt until there are no lumps remaining.

2 Melt the ghee in a kadhai, wok, or heavy-bottom pan over medium-high heat. Mix in the yogurt mixture and then the water, whisking constantly. Bring to a boil, then reduce the heat to very low and simmer, still whisking frequently, for 8 minutes, or until the soup thickens slightly and no longer has a "raw" taste. Taste and add extra salt, if necessary.

3 Melt the ghee for the garnish in a small pan. Add the cumin, mustard, and fenugreek seeds and cook, stirring, until the seeds start to crackle and jump. Add the chilies, then remove from the heat and stir for 30 seconds, or until the chilies blister (if the chilies are fresh, they might burst and jump, so stand well back).

4 To serve, ladle the soup into warmed bowls and spoon the fried spices over, including a little of the light brown ghee.

Tunisian Garlic and Chickpea Soup

The mellow flavor of garlic is complemented by the warm spices in this rich and substantial soup.

SERVES 4

PREP TIME 15 MINUTES, PLUS 8 HOURS' SOAKING

COOKING TIME 2¾ HOURS

8 tbsp olive oil

12 garlic cloves, very finely chopped

3 cups chickpeas, soaked overnight in cold water and drained

2½ quarts water

1 tsp ground cumin

1 tsp ground coriander

2 carrots, very finely chopped

2 onions, very finely chopped

6 celery stalks, very finely chopped

juice of 1 lemon

4 tbsp chopped fresh cilantro, plus extra sprigs to garnish

salt and pepper

1 Heat half the oil in a large, heavy-bottom pan over low heat. Add the garlic and cook, stirring frequently, for 2 minutes. Add the drained chickpeas, water, cumin, and ground coriander. Bring to a boil, then reduce the heat and simmer for 2½ hours, or until tender.

2 Meanwhile, heat the remaining oil in a separate pan. Add the carrots, onions, and celery, then cover and cook over medium-low heat, stirring occasionally, for 20 minutes.

3 Stir the vegetable mixture into the pan of chickpeas. Transfer about half the soup to a food processor or blender and process until smooth. Return the purée to the pan, then add about half the lemon juice and stir. Taste and add more lemon juice, if necessary. Season to taste with salt and pepper and heat through. Ladle into warmed bowls and sprinkle with the chopped fresh cilantro, then garnish with cilantro sprigs and serve.

Gazpacho

This is one of the classic chilled soups, originating from Andalusia in southern Spain, and is as refreshing as fruit juice on a hot summer's day.

SERVES 4–6

PREP TIME 20 MINUTES, PLUS 4 HOURS' CHILLING

COOKING TIME NO COOKING

1 lb 2 oz/500 g large, juicy tomatoes, peeled, seeded, and chopped

3 large, ripe red bell peppers, seeded and chopped

about 2 tbsp sherry vinegar

4 tbsp olive oil

pinch of sugar

salt and pepper

to serve

ice cubes

finely diced red bell pepper

finely diced green bell pepper

finely diced yellow bell pepper

finely diced seeded cucumber

finely chopped hard-cooked eggs

croutons fried in garlic-flavored olive oil

1 Put the tomatoes, red bell peppers, 2 tablespoons of vinegar, the oil, sugar, and salt and pepper to taste in a food processor or blender and process until blended and as smooth or chunky as you like. Cover and chill for at least 4 hours before serving. Taste and adjust the seasoning, adding extra vinegar if necessary.

2 To serve, ladle the soup into chilled bowls and add 1 or 2 ice cubes to each. Put the diced bell peppers and cucumber, eggs, and croutons in bowls and let everyone add what they like.

Chef's tip

Cold dulls flavors, so more seasoning will be needed than for a soup served warm. For this reason, taste and adjust the seasoning after chilling the soup.

Shrimp Laksa

This creamy soup, with rice vermicelli noodles and lightly cooked shrimp, combines wonderful Thai flavors to create a dish that is both warming and satisfying.

SERVES 4

PREP TIME 10 MINUTES

COOKING TIME 10 MINUTES

1¾ cups canned coconut milk

1¼ cups vegetable stock

1¾ oz/50 g rice vermicelli noodles

1 red bell pepper, seeded and cut into strips

8 oz/225 g canned bamboo shoots, drained and rinsed

2-inch/5-cm piece fresh gingerroot, thinly sliced

3 scallions, chopped

1 tbsp red Thai curry paste

2 tbsp Thai fish sauce

1 tsp palm sugar or soft light brown sugar

6 fresh Thai basil sprigs

12 cooked unshelled shrimp

1 Pour the coconut milk and stock into a pan and bring slowly to a boil. Add all the remaining ingredients, except the shrimp, then reduce the heat and simmer gently for 4–5 minutes, or until the noodles are tender.

2 Add the shrimp and simmer for an additional 1–2 minutes, or until heated through. Ladle the soup into small warmed bowls, dividing the shrimp between them, and serve.

Chef's tip

Serve the soup immediately, as the noodles will continue to swell and soak up all the liquid.

Borscht

Antonin Carême, chef to Czar Alexander I, is credited with introducing this traditional Russian beet soup to France and so to the rest of Europe. This is a lighter, easier version of his rather elaborate recipe and is suitable for vegetarians.

SERVES 6

PREP TIME 30 MINUTES

COOKING TIME 1¼ HOURS

1 onion

½ stick salted/unsalted butter

12 oz/350 g raw beet, cut into thin sticks, and

1 raw beet, grated

1 carrot, cut into

thin sticks

3 celery stalks, thinly sliced

2 tomatoes, peeled,

seeded, and chopped

5¾ cups vegetable stock

1 tbsp white wine vinegar

1 tbsp sugar

2 large fresh dill sprigs, snipped

1 cup shredded white cabbage

salt and pepper

⅔ cup sour cream, to garnish

rye bread, to serve (optional)

1 Slice the onion into rings. Melt the butter in a large, heavy-bottom pan over low heat. Add the onion and cook, stirring occasionally, for 3–5 minutes, or until softened. Add the beet sticks, carrot, celery, and tomatoes. Cook, stirring frequently, for 4–5 minutes.

2 Add the stock, vinegar, sugar, and a tablespoon of dill to the pan. Season to taste with salt and pepper. Bring to a boil, then reduce the heat and simmer for 35–40 minutes, or until the vegetables are tender.

3 Stir in the cabbage, then cover and simmer for 10 minutes. Stir in the grated beet, with any juices, and cook for an additional 10 minutes. Ladle into warmed bowls. Garnish with a spoonful of sour cream and the remaining snipped dill, and serve with rye bread, if liked.

Aromatic Chicken and Vegetable Soup

This Asian soup is typically light and fragrant, with a hint of chili. It is also full of textural interest, with its lively mix of fresh vegetables.

SERVES 4

PREP TIME 15 MINUTES

COOKING TIME 30 MINUTES

handful of fresh cilantro

4 cups chicken stock

1 fresh lemongrass stem, bruised

1 small fresh red chili

grated rind and juice of ½ lime

8 oz/225 g skinless, boneless chicken breast, diced

1 cup snow peas, cut diagonally into thin strips

1 carrot, shaved into ribbons

3½ oz/100 g baby corn, thinly sliced, or corn

4 scallions, thinly sliced, plus extra fine strips to garnish (optional)

salt and pepper

1 Strip the cilantro leaves from the stems. Reserve the leaves and put the stems in a large pan with the stock, lemongrass, chili, and lime rind. Bring to a boil, then reduce the heat and simmer, covered, for 15 minutes.

2 Strain the stock into a separate pan and discard the flavorings. Add the lime juice and salt and pepper to taste.

3 Add the chicken to the stock. Bring to a boil, then reduce the heat and simmer for 5 minutes. Add the snow peas, carrot, and baby corn and simmer for 2 minutes, or until the vegetables are tender and the chicken is cooked through.

4 Coarsely chop the cilantro leaves and stir into the soup with the scallions. Serve immediately in warmed bowls, garnished with fine scallion strips, if liked.

Scotch Broth

This Scottish soup is actually a nourishing one-pot meal in itself, as it contains lamb, lots of vegetables, and pearl barley. Because lamb is quite a fatty meat, it is a good idea to make this soup the day before to enable the excess fat to solidify and be removed.

SERVES 6–8

PREP TIME 20 MINUTES, PLUS
9 HOURS' COOLING AND CHILLING

COOKING TIME 2¼ HOURS

1 lb 9 oz/700 g neck of lamb

6¾ cups water

scant ⅓ cup pearl barley

2 onions, chopped

1 garlic clove, finely chopped

3 small turnips, finely diced

3 carrots, thinly sliced

2 celery stalks, sliced

2 leeks, sliced

salt and pepper

2 tbsp chopped fresh parsley, to garnish

1 Cut the meat into small pieces, removing as much fat as possible. Put in a large pan, then cover with the water and bring to a boil over medium heat, skimming off any scum that rises to the surface.

2 Add the pearl barley, then reduce the heat and simmer gently, covered, for 1 hour.

3 Add the prepared vegetables and season well with salt and pepper. Continue to cook for an additional hour. Remove from the heat and let cool slightly.

4 Remove the meat from the pan with a slotted spoon and strip the meat from the bones. Discard the bones and any fat or gristle. Return the meat to the pan and let cool completely, then cover and let chill overnight.

5 Scrape the solidified fat off the surface of the soup. Reheat, then season to taste with salt and pepper and serve piping hot, with the parsley scattered over the top.

Middle Eastern Soup with Harissa

Harissa is a fiery-hot chili sauce from Tunisia. This version perfectly complements the succulent lamb soup, but it is also ideal with couscous and in stews.

SERVES 6

PREP TIME 30 MINUTES, PLUS 15 MINUTES' COOLING

COOKING TIME 1½ HOURS

2 eggplants

4 chilies

3 tbsp olive oil

6 lamb shanks

1 small onion, chopped

1¾ cups chicken stock

8 cups water

14 oz/400 g sweet potato, cut into chunks

2-inch/5-cm piece cinnamon stick

1 tsp ground cumin

2 tbsp chopped fresh cilantro

harissa

2 red bell peppers, roasted, peeled, seeded, and chopped

½ tsp coriander seeds, dry-fried

1 oz/25 g fresh red chilies, chopped

2 garlic cloves, chopped

2 tsp caraway seeds

olive oil

salt

1 Preheat the oven to 400°F/200°C. Prick the eggplants and chilies and put on a cookie sheet and bake in the oven for 1 hour. When cool enough to handle, peel and chop the eggplants.

2 Meanwhile, heat the oil in a pan. Add the shanks and cook until browned all over. Add the onion, stock, and water. Bring to a boil, then reduce the heat and simmer for 1 hour.

3 For the harissa, put the red bell peppers, coriander seeds, chilies, garlic, and caraway seeds in a food processor and process until well blended. With the motor running, add enough oil through the feed tube to make a paste. Season to taste with salt, then spoon into a screw-top jar. Cover with a layer of oil, then screw on the lid and chill until required.

4 Remove the shanks from the stock, then cut off the meat and chop. Add the sweet potato, cinnamon, and cumin to the stock and bring to a boil. Reduce the heat, then cover and simmer for 20 minutes. Discard the cinnamon. Transfer the mixture to a food processor or blender with the eggplant and process until smooth. Return to the pan, then add the lamb, chilies, and fresh cilantro and heat through. Serve with the harissa.

Chef's tip

Make this soup and the harissa the day before to guarantee the maximum amount of flavor.

Spicy Beef and Noodle Soup

This meaty Thai soup with noodles is a wonderful appetizer, but it can also make a satisfying light lunch or supper in itself.

SERVES 4

PREP TIME 10 MINUTES

COOKING TIME 10 MINUTES

4 cups beef stock

⅔ cup vegetable or peanut oil

3 oz/85 g rice vermicelli noodles

2 shallots, thinly sliced

2 garlic cloves, crushed

1-inch/2.5-cm piece fresh gingerroot, thinly sliced

1 tenderloin, about 8 oz/225 g, cut into thin strips

2 tbsp green Thai curry paste

2 tbsp Thai soy sauce

1 tbsp Thai fish sauce

chopped fresh cilantro, to garnish

1 Pour the stock into a large pan and bring to a boil. Meanwhile, heat the oil in a preheated wok or large skillet over high heat. Add a third of the noodles and fry for 30 seconds, or until crisp and puffed up. Remove with tongs, then drain on paper towels and set aside. Discard all but 2 tablespoons of the oil.

2 Add the shallots, garlic, and ginger to the wok or skillet and stir-fry for 1 minute. Add the beef and curry paste and stir-fry for an additional 3–4 minutes, or until tender.

3 Transfer the beef mixture, the uncooked noodles, soy sauce, and fish sauce to the pan of stock and simmer for 2–3 minutes, or until the noodles have swelled. Serve hot, garnished with cilantro and the reserved crispy noodles.

Khandvi

Served at weddings and various religious festivals in India, these delicate gram flour rolls make an appetizing canapé with cocktails or dry white wine.

MAKES 16 ROLLS

PREP TIME 20 MINUTES, PLUS 30 MINUTES' COOLING TIME

COOKING TIME 35 MINUTES

generous ½ cup gram flour

1 tsp ground ginger

1 tsp salt

½ tsp ground turmeric

¼ tsp chili powder, or to taste

scant 2 cups water

¾ cup plain yogurt

1 tbsp lemon juice

vegetable oil, for oiling

to garnish

2 tbsp vegetable or peanut oil

½ tbsp black mustard seeds

½ tbsp sesame seeds, toasted

1 fresh green chili, seeded and finely chopped (optional)

½ tbsp finely chopped fresh cilantro

1 Sift the gram flour, ginger, salt, turmeric, and chili powder together into a bowl and make a well in the center. Whisk the water, yogurt, and lemon juice together, then pour into the well and whisk until a smooth batter forms.

2 Rinse the widest and deepest pan you have with cold water, then pour in the batter. Put over high heat and bring to a boil, stirring constantly. Reduce the heat and continue to simmer and stir for 30 minutes, or until the liquid evaporates and the mixture is thick.

3 Meanwhile, lightly oil a shallow, square 12-inch/30-cm baking sheet. Pour the mixture into the baking sheet and use a wet spatula to spread it out about ⅛ inch/3 mm thick. Alternatively, spread the mixture out on a clean counter to a 12 inch/30 cm square of the same thickness. Set aside and let cool completely.

4 Use a sharp knife to cut the mixture into 8 strips, each 1½ inches/ 4 cm wide, then cut each strip in half so that it is 6 inches/15 cm long. Use a round-bladed knife to lift up the strips, then roll them up like a jelly roll. Transfer the rolls to a serving platter and chill until required.

5 Just before serving, heat the oil in a pan or skillet over medium heat. Add the mustard and sesame seeds and cook, stirring constantly, until they start to crackle and jump. Immediately remove from the heat, then add the chili, if using, and stir for 30 seconds, then pour the oil and spices over the rolls. Sprinkle with the cilantro and serve.

Tropical Fruit Salad

While northerners shiver through the cold winter months and comfort themselves with warming stews and casseroles, Floridians feast on fresh fruit salads. The use of fresh lime and chili gives this example a Latino flavor from Miami.

SERVES 4

PREP TIME 15 MINUTES, PLUS 1 HOUR'S CHILLING

COOKING TIME NO COOKING

1 large ripe mango

2 large oranges

1 pink grapefruit

1 tsp finely grated lime rind

4 tbsp fresh lime juice, or to taste

1 fresh red chili, seeded and finely sliced

4 tbsp grated fresh coconut or dry unsweetened coconut

chopped fresh cilantro, to garnish

1 To prepare the mango, slice it lengthwise on either side of the flat central seed. Peel the 2 mango pieces and cut the flesh into chunks. Slice off and peel any remaining flesh around the seed, then cut into chunks and put in a nonmetallic bowl.

2 Peel the oranges and grapefruit, carefully removing all the bitter white pith. As each fruit is peeled, separate it into segments over the bowl of mango, cutting between the membranes and letting the segments drop into the bowl. Squeeze the juice from the membranes into the bowl.

3 Stir the lime rind, lime juice, chili, and coconut into the bowl. Cover and chill for at least 1 hour to let the flavors blend.

4 Stir the fruit salad and add extra lime juice, if necessary. Spoon into 4 bowls and sprinkle with cilantro to garnish.

Chef's tip

This is a mix-and-match salad that is equally good with whatever fresh tropical fruit is available—try pineapple, carambola, papaya, and even avocado. It's a refreshing first course as it is, but for a more substantial dish, add poached shrimp or crabmeat, or serve with cottage cheese.

Tempura

Japanese tempura is a dish of vegetables and pieces of fish coated in batter and deep-fried. This version, with its delicious dipping sauce, is suitable for vegetarians.

SERVES 4

PREP TIME 15 MINUTES

COOKING TIME 25 MINUTES

5½-oz/150-g package tempura mix

4 shiitake mushrooms

4 fresh asparagus spears

4 slices sweet potato

1 red bell pepper, seeded and cut into strips

4 slices onion, cut widthwise into rings

vegetable or peanut oil, for deep-frying

dipping sauce

2 tsp mirin

1 tbsp shoyu (Japanese soy sauce)

pinch of dashi granules, dissolved in 2 tbsp boiling water

1 For the dipping sauce, mix all the ingredients together in a small dipping dish.

2 Mix the tempura with water according to the package directions. Don't try to make the batter smooth—it should be a little lumpy. Drop the vegetables into the batter.

3 Fill a preheated wok two-thirds full with oil, or use a deep-fat fryer. Heat the oil to 350–375°F/180–190°C, or until a cube of bread browns in 30 seconds. Lift 2–3 pieces of tempura out of the batter, then add to the oil and cook for 2–3 minutes, or until lightly golden brown. Remove with a slotted spoon, then drain on paper towels and keep hot while you cook the remaining tempura pieces. Serve with the dipping sauce.

Chef's tip

Do not cook more than two or three pieces of tempura at a time, otherwise the oil temperature will drop and the tempura will be soggy. If you prefer, you can use ordinary potato in place of the sweet potato.

Mediterranean Split Pea Dip

This popular meze dish is similar to hummus, but made with yellow split peas. It is simple to make, and yet even easier if whizzed up in a food processor or blender.

Serves 6
Prep Time 15 minutes
Cooking Time 50 minutes

1¼ cups yellow split peas
2 small onions, 1 coarsely chopped and
1 very finely chopped
1 garlic clove, coarsely chopped
6 tbsp extra virgin olive oil
1 tbsp chopped fresh oregano, plus extra to
garnish (optional)
salt and pepper
savory biscuits, to serve

1 Rinse the split peas under cold running water. Put in a pan and add the coarsely chopped onion, the garlic, and plenty of cold water. Bring to a boil, then reduce the heat and simmer for 45 minutes, or until very tender.

2 Drain the split peas, reserving a little of the cooking liquid, and put in a food processor or blender. Add 5 tablespoons of the oil and process until smooth. If the mixture seems too dry, add enough of the reserved liquid to form a smooth, thick purée. Alternatively, mash the split peas with a fork in a bowl. Add the oregano and season to taste with salt and pepper.

3 Turn the mixture into a serving bowl and sprinkle with the finely chopped onion and extra oregano, if liked. Drizzle over the remaining oil. Serve warm or cold with savory biscuits.

# Guacamole

Making a good guacamole means using high-quality, ripe avocados. Mashing rather than puréeing gives control over the texture. Served with tortilla chips, this Mexican relish teams well with sour cream and salsa.

SERVES 4

PREP TIME 15 MINUTES

COOKING TIME NO COOKING

2 large ripe avocados

juice of 1 lime

2 tsp olive oil

½ onion, finely chopped

1 fresh green chili, such as poblano, seeded and finely chopped

1 garlic clove, crushed

¼ tsp ground cumin

1 tbsp chopped fresh cilantro, plus extra sprigs to garnish (optional)

salt and pepper

1 Cut each avocado in half lengthwise and twist the 2 halves in opposite directions to separate. Stab the pit of each avocado with the point of a sharp knife, then lift out and discard.

2 Peel, then coarsely chop the avocado halves and put in a nonmetallic bowl. Squeeze over the lime juice and add the oil.

3 Mash the avocados with a fork until the desired consistency—either chunky or smooth—is reached. Blend in the onion, chili, garlic, cumin, and cilantro, then season to taste with salt and pepper.

4 Transfer to a serving dish and serve immediately, to avoid discoloration, garnished with cilantro sprigs, if liked.

Vegetarian Samosas

It takes a little practice and patience to get the hang of shaping these triangular-shaped pastries, but after you've rolled out and filled a couple, you will become as proficient as India's many street cooks. Samosas are fried and sold at every street market and busy intersection.

MAKES 14

PREP TIME 30 MINUTES, PLUS 15 MINUTES' RESTING

COOKING TIME 45 MINUTES

1⅔ cups all-purpose flour

½ tsp salt

3 tbsp ghee or salted/unsalted butter, melted

½ tbsp lemon juice

scant ¼–½ cup cold water

filling

4 tbsp ghee or 4 tbsp vegetable oil

1 onion, very finely chopped

2 garlic cloves, crushed

1 potato, very finely diced

2 carrots, very finely chopped

2 tsp mild, medium, or hot curry powder, to taste

1½ tsp ground coriander

1 tsp ground turmeric

1 fresh green chili, seeded and finely chopped

1 tsp salt

½ tsp black mustard seeds

1¼ cups water

1 cup frozen peas

2 oz/55 g cauliflower, broken into very small florets

vegetable or peanut oil, for frying

1 For the filling, melt the ghee in a kadhai, wok, or large skillet over medium-high heat. Add the onion and garlic and cook, stirring frequently, for 5–8 minutes, or until softened but not browned. Stir in the potato and carrots and cook, stirring occasionally, for 5 minutes. Stir in the curry powder, coriander, turmeric, chili, salt, and mustard seeds. Pour in the water and bring to a boil. Reduce the heat to very low and simmer, uncovered, for 15 minutes, stirring occasionally. Add the peas and cauliflower florets and simmer until all the vegetables are tender and the liquid evaporates. Remove from the heat and set aside.

2 Meanwhile, for the pastry, sift the flour and salt into a bowl. Make a well in the center, then add the ghee and lemon juice and work them into the flour with your fingertips. Gradually add the water until the mixture comes together to form a soft dough. Tip the dough onto the counter and knead for about 10 minutes until smooth. Shape into a ball, then cover and let rest for about 15 minutes. Divide into 7 equal pieces. Roll each into an 8-inch/20-cm circle on a lightly greased counter, then cut in half to make 2 equal semicircles. Wet the edges and place about 2 teaspoons of the filling on each piece, just off center. Fold in the sides to form a cone shape and seal with water.

3 Heat about 1 inch/2.5 cm of oil in a large, heavy-bottom pan to 350–375°F/180–190°C, or until a cube of bread browns in 30 seconds. Add the samosas, in batches, to the oil and cook for 2–3 minutes, turning once, until golden brown. Remove with a slotted spoon, then drain on paper towels and keep warm while you cook the remaining samosas.

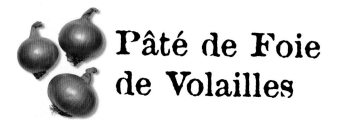

Pâté de Foie de Volailles

The richness of this smooth, elegant version of chicken liver pâté belies its simplicity. In French bistros, it is served with a crock of cornichons, a basket of French bread, and pots of unsalted butter for spreading on the bread with the pâté.

MAKES 8–10 SLICES

PREP TIME 15 MINUTES, PLUS 30 MINUTES' COOLING

COOKING TIME 10 MINUTES

1½ sticks unsalted butter

1 lb 2 oz/500 g chicken livers, thawed if frozen, trimmed

½ tbsp corn or sunflower-seed oil

2 shallots, finely chopped

2 large garlic cloves, finely chopped

2½ tbsp Madeira or brandy

2 tbsp heavy cream

1 tsp dried thyme

¼ tsp ground allspice

salt and pepper

chopped fresh flat-leaf parsley, to garnish

to serve

toasted slices brioche

mixed salad greens tossed with French dressing

1 Melt 2 tbsp of the butter in a large sauté pan or skillet over medium-high heat. Add the chicken livers and cook, stirring, for 5 minutes, or until brown on the outside, but still slightly pink in the centers. Work in batches, if necessary, to avoid overcrowding the pan.

2 Transfer the livers and their cooking juices to a food processor or blender. Melt another 2 tbsp of the remaining butter with the oil in the pan. Add the shallots and garlic and cook, stirring frequently, for 2–3 minutes, or until the shallots are softened but not browned.

3 Add the Madeira to the pan and scrape up any cooking juices from the base. Stir in the cream, then stir in the thyme, allspice, and salt and pepper to taste. Transfer the mixture to the food processor or blender with the livers, adding all the cooking juices. Add the remaining butter, cut into small pieces.

4 Process the mixture until smooth. Taste and adjust the seasoning, if necessary. Let the mixture cool slightly, then scrape into a serving bowl and set aside to let the pâté cool completely.

5 When the pâté is cool, it can be served immediately, or covered with plastic wrap and chilled for up to 3 days. Let stand at room temperature for 30 minutes before serving. Just before serving, sprinkle the pâté with parsley to garnish, then serve with toasted brioche and dressed mixed salad greens.

Blinis

Blinis come from Russia. Traditionally, these small yeast pancakes are made with buckwheat flour, which gives them a tasty and unusual flavor. This recipe preserves that tradition. You can also serve these pancakes with caviar.

MAKES 8 BLINIS

PREP TIME 20 MINUTES, PLUS 1 HOUR'S STANDING

COOKING TIME 20 MINUTES

¾ cup buckwheat flour

generous ⅔ cup strong white bread flour

⅙-oz/7-g sachet active dry yeast

1 tsp salt

1½ cups tepid milk

2 eggs, 1 whole and 1 separated

vegetable oil, for brushing

to serve

sour cream

smoked salmon

1 Sift both flours into a large, warmed bowl. Stir in the yeast and salt. Beat in the milk, the whole egg, and egg yolk until smooth. Cover the bowl and let stand in a warm place for 1 hour.

2 Put the egg white in a spotlessly clean bowl and whisk until soft peaks form. Fold into the batter. Brush a heavy-bottom skillet with oil and heat over medium-high heat. When the skillet is hot, pour enough of the batter onto the surface to make a blini about the size of a saucer.

3 When bubbles rise, turn the blini over with a spatula and cook the other side until light brown. Wrap in a clean dish towel to keep warm while you cook the remaining blinis. Serve the warm blinis with sour cream and smoked salmon.

Polenta with Prosciutto

These tasty Italian-style morsels are ideal appetizers when you are entertaining, as they can be prepared in advance and then popped under the broiler when you are ready to serve.

SERVES 6

PREP TIME 15 MINUTES, PLUS 30 MINUTES' COOLING

COOKING TIME 20 MINUTES

2 tbsp extra virgin olive oil, plus extra for oiling

2½ cups water

large pinch of salt

scant ⅓ cup quick-cook polenta

¼ cup freshly grated Parmesan cheese

2 tbsp butter, softened

salt and pepper

topping

6 slices prosciutto crudo

3 oz/85 g fontina cheese, cut into 6 slices

12 fresh sage leaves

extra virgin olive oil, plus extra for dipping

salt and pepper

1 Line a 6-x-10-inch/15-x-25-cm jelly roll pan with parchment paper and set aside. Oil a cookie sheet.

2 Pour the water into a large pan and bring to a boil. Reduce the heat so that it is just simmering and add the salt. Add the polenta in a steady stream, stirring constantly. Simmer, stirring constantly, for 5 minutes, or until thickened.

3 Remove from the heat. Stir in the Parmesan cheese and butter and season to taste with pepper. Spoon the polenta evenly into the pan and smooth the surface with a spatula. Set aside to cool completely.

4 Turn out the polenta, keeping its shape. Using an oiled 3-inch/7.5-cm plain, round pastry cutter, stamp out 6 circles and put on the cookie sheet. Brush with a little oil and season to taste with salt and pepper.

5 Cook under a preheated broiler for 3–4 minutes. Turn the circles over, then brush with the remaining oil and cook for an additional 3–4 minutes, or until golden. Remove from the broiler and, if you are not serving immediately, set the circles aside to cool completely.

6 Drape a slice of ham on each polenta circle and top with a slice of fontina cheese. Brush the sage leaves with olive oil and put 2 on each polenta circle. Cook the polenta circles under a preheated broiler for 3–4 minutes until the cheese has melted and the sage is crisp. Serve immediately with extra oil for dipping.

Jiaozi

These crescent-shaped dumplings are extremely popular in central and northern China and bear a time-honored history, moving from the status of a common snack to a specialty dish associated with festivals. They originated from won tons.

MAKES ABOUT 50 JIAOZI

PREP TIME 40 MINUTES, PLUS 20 MINUTES' RESTING

COOKING TIME 35 MINUTES

1 lb/450 g fresh ground pork, not too lean

1 tbsp light soy sauce

1½ tsp salt

1 tsp Shaoxing rice wine

½ tsp sesame oil

3½ oz/100 g cabbage, very finely chopped

2 tsp finely chopped fresh gingerroot

2 tsp finely chopped scallion

½ tsp white pepper

50 round won ton skins, about 2¾ inches/7 cm in diameter

all-purpose flour, for dusting

chili or soy dipping sauce, to serve

1 For the filling, mix the pork with the soy sauce and ½ teaspoon of the salt. Stir carefully, always in the same direction, to create a thick paste. Add the rice wine and oil and continue mixing in the same direction. Cover and let rest for at least 20 minutes.

2 To prepare the cabbage, sprinkle with the remaining salt to help draw out the water. Add the ginger, scallion, and pepper and knead for at least 5 minutes into a thick paste. Combine with the filling.

3 To make the dumplings, put about 1 tablespoon of the filling in the center of each skin, holding the skin in the palm of one hand. Moisten the edges with water, then seal the edges with 2 or 3 pleats on each side and transfer to a lightly floured board.

4 To cook the dumplings, bring 4 cups water to a rolling boil in a large pan or stockpot. Drop in about 20 dumplings at a time, stirring gently with a chopstick to prevent them sticking together. Cover, then return to a boil and cook for 2 minutes. Uncover and add a generous ¾ cup cold water. Return to a boil, then cover and cook for an additional 2 minutes. Remove with a slotted spoon and keep hot while you cook the remaining jiaozi. Serve with the dipping sauce.

Fish and Shellfish

The seafood dishes in this chapter look very impressive, but are surprisingly quick and easy to make.

Moroccan Red Snapper with Chermoula

Chermoula is a special Moroccan mix of garlic, coriander, and spices. The fish is marinated in this exotic mixture before being broiled or cooked on the grill.

SERVES 4

PREP TIME 20 MINUTES, PLUS 1 HOUR'S MARINATING

COOKING TIME 8–10 MINUTES

4 garlic cloves

pinch of sea salt

scant 1 cup chopped fresh cilantro, plus extra sprigs to garnish

2 tsp paprika

2 tsp ground cumin

pinch of chili powder

⅔ cup olive oil, plus extra for oiling

4 tbsp lemon or lime juice

red snapper or pompano, either 4 fish x 12 oz/350 g each, or 8 fish x 6 oz/175 g, cleaned and scaled

lime wedges, to garnish

1 For the chermoula, pound the garlic with the sea salt in a mortar with a pestle. Gradually work in the cilantro and spices. Transfer to a bowl and gradually whisk in the oil, then the lemon juice.

2 Make 3–4 diagonal slashes on both sides of the fish. Rub the chermoula into the slashes. Put the fish in a nonmetallic dish, then cover and let marinate in the refrigerator for 1 hour.

3 Preheat the broiler or gas grill to high, or light grill coals. Put the fish onto an oiled broiler rack or grill grid and cook under the broiler or over the grill for 4–5 minutes on each side until the flesh flakes easily. Serve immediately, garnished with cilantro sprigs and lime wedges.

Mexican-Style Fish with a Chili Crust

This attractive and flavor-packed dish can be made with any firm-fleshed fish, such as tuna, cod, or angler fish.

SERVES 4

PREP TIME 10 MINUTES

COOKING TIME 10 MINUTES

1 small bunch fresh cilantro or flat-leaf parsley

3–4 dried red chilies, crushed

2 tbsp sesame seeds

1 egg white

4 tuna steaks, about 5–6 oz/140–175 g each

2–3 tbsp corn or sunflower-seed oil

2 limes, halved, to garnish

salt and pepper

1 Chop the cilantro, reserving a few whole sprigs to garnish. Mix the crushed chilies, chopped cilantro, and sesame seeds together in a shallow dish and season to taste with salt and pepper. Lightly beat the egg white with a fork in a separate shallow dish.

2 Dip the tuna steaks first in the egg white, then in the chili and herb mixture to coat. Gently pat the crust evenly over the steaks with the palm of your hand, making sure that both sides are well covered.

3 Heat the oil in a large, heavy-bottom skillet over medium heat. Add the steaks and cook for 4 minutes, then turn over carefully with a spatula. Cook for an additional 4 minutes, then transfer to warmed serving plates. Garnish with the lime halves and reserved cilantro sprigs and serve immediately.

Sicilian Tuna

This quick, spicy dish can be cooked in the kitchen or on the grill. It needs nothing more than a crisp salad as an accompaniment.

SERVES 4

PREP TIME 15 MINUTES, PLUS 30 MINUTES' MARINATING

COOKING TIME 15 MINUTES

2 fennel bulbs, thickly sliced lengthwise

2 red onions, sliced

2 tbsp virgin olive oil

4 tuna steaks, about 5 oz/140 g each

crisp green salad, to serve

marinade

½ cup extra virgin olive oil

4 garlic cloves, finely chopped

4 fresh red chilies, seeded and finely chopped

juice and finely grated rind of 2 lemons

4 tbsp finely chopped fresh flat-leaf parsley

salt and pepper

1 Whisk all the ingredients for the marinade together in a bowl. Put the tuna steaks in a large, shallow dish and spoon over 4 tablespoons of the marinade, turning to coat. Cover and let marinate in the refrigerator for 30 minutes. Set aside the remaining marinade.

2 Preheat a ridged grill pan over medium-high heat. Put the fennel and onions in a bowl, then add the oil and toss well to coat. Add to the grill pan and cook for 5 minutes on each side, or until beginning to color. Transfer to 4 warmed serving plates, then drizzle with the reserved marinade and keep warm while you cook the tuna steaks.

3 Add the tuna steaks to the grill pan and cook, turning once, for 4–5 minutes, or until firm to the touch but still moist inside. Transfer the tuna to the plates and serve immediately with a crisp green salad.

Traditional Greek Baked Fish

The traditional way of baking fish in Greece is whole with tomatoes and lemons (which are eaten with the rind on), although both the Greeks and the Turks claim to have originated the method. A variety of fish can be cooked in this way, so choose from the suggestions in the recipe.

SERVES 4–6

PREP TIME 20 MINUTES

COOKING TIME 1 HOUR 25–40 MINUTES

5 tbsp olive oil, plus extra for oiling

2 onions, thinly sliced

2 garlic cloves, finely chopped

2 carrots, thinly sliced

2 celery stalks, thinly sliced

⅔ cup dry white wine

14 oz/400 g canned chopped tomatoes in juice

pinch of sugar

1 large lemon, thinly sliced

2 tbsp chopped fresh flat-leaf parsley

1 tsp chopped fresh marjoram

1 fat whole fish, about 2 lb 4 oz–3 lb/1–1.3 kg, such as bass, tilapia or red snapper, cleaned and scaled

salt and pepper

1 Preheat the oven to 350°F/180°C. Oil a shallow ovenproof dish. Heat 4 tablespoons of the oil in a large pan over medium heat. Add the onions and garlic and cook, stirring frequently, for 5 minutes, or until softened. Add the carrots and celery and cook, stirring frequently, for 8–10 minutes, or until slightly softened.

2 Pour the wine into the pan and bring to a boil. Add the tomatoes with their juice, sugar, lemon slices, and salt and pepper to taste and simmer for 20 minutes. Stir in the herbs.

3 Put the fish in the ovenproof dish. Pour the vegetables around the fish, arranging some of the lemon slices on top. Sprinkle with the remaining oil and season to taste with salt and pepper.

4 Bake the fish, uncovered, in the oven for 45 minutes–1 hour, depending on the thickness of the fish, until tender. Serve immediately.

Sweet Chili Salmon Sushi Rolls

These Japanese sushi rolls make delicious use of crisply fried salmon skin. Sweet chili sauce is available in many different brands. The best are Thai brands, available from Chinese and Thai stores.

MAKES 6 ROLLS

PREP TIME 20 MINUTES, PLUS 30 MINUTES' COOLING

COOKING TIME 8 MINUTES, EXCLUDING COOKING THE RICE

1 skin-on salmon fillet, about 5½ oz/150 g

1 tbsp vegetable or peanut oil

3 large sheets toasted nori, halved

¾ cup freshly cooked sushi rice

2 scallions, halved and shredded

4 tbsp Japanese mayonnaise

2 tbsp sweet chili sauce, plus extra to serve

salt and pepper

thin cucumber sticks, to serve

1 Season the salmon to taste with salt and pepper. Heat the oil in a skillet over high heat. When very hot, add the salmon, skin-side down, and cook for 2 minutes, or until the skin is very crisp. Reduce the heat to medium and cook for an additional 2 minutes. Turn the salmon over and cook for an additional minute, or until it is cooked through. Remove from the skillet and let cool. Flake the salmon, keeping some pieces attached to the crispy skin.

2 Lay a piece of nori out on the counter and put some rice on the sheet. Spread the rice out evenly so that it takes up the bottom two-thirds of the sheet. Lay a sixth of the salmon, salmon skin, and scallions on the rice, then drizzle over a little mayonnaise and dot on a tiny amount of the sweet chili sauce. Roll the nori into a cone, folding the bottom corner in as you roll. Paste the join together with a couple of crushed grains of rice. Repeat with the remaining ingredients.

3 Serve the sushi rolls with cucumber sticks and sweet chili sauce, for dipping.

Asian Rainbow Trout

Rainbow trout has a flaky texture and a delicate taste that combines beautifully with the Asian flavors of lemongrass, coconut, fresh ginger, and cilantro leaves.

SERVES 4

PREP TIME 15 MINUTES

COOKING TIME 5–6 MINUTES

4 rainbow trout fillets, about 6 oz/175 g each

4 tbsp chili oil

2 tbsp lemon juice

1 garlic clove, finely chopped

1 tbsp finely grated fresh gingerroot

1 tbsp freshly grated lemongrass

1 tbsp chopped fresh cilantro, plus extra sprigs to garnish

salt and pepper

grated fresh coconut, to garnish

boiled rice, to serve

1 Rinse the fish fillets under cold running water, then pat dry with paper towels.

2 Brush a shallow heatproof dish with a little of the oil, then arrange the fish in it. Season the fish to taste with salt and pepper.

3 Preheat the broiler to medium. Mix the remaining oil, lemon juice, garlic, ginger, lemongrass, and chopped cilantro together in a bowl. Spread the mixture all over the fish, then transfer the dish to the broiler. Cook under the broiler, turning once, for 5–6 minutes, or until the fish is cooked through.

4 Remove the dish from the broiler. Remove the fillets from the dish with a spatula and arrange on individual warmed serving plates. Pour over the cooking juices from the dish, then garnish with cilantro sprigs and grated coconut and serve with boiled rice.

Fish Curry with Rice Noodles

This aromatic Thai dish uses angler fish, salmon, and cod. Angler fish used to be a much underrated fish, but nowadays the tail flesh is becoming increasingly prized for its lean, firm texture, pearly color, and sweet flavor.

SERVES 4

PREP TIME 20 MINUTES

COOKING TIME 10 MINUTES

2 tbsp vegetable or peanut oil

1 large onion, chopped

2 garlic cloves, chopped

1½ cups white mushrooms

8 oz/225 g angler fish, cut into 1-inch/2.5-cm cubes

8 oz/225 g salmon fillets, cut into 1-inch/2.5-cm cubes

8 oz/225 g cod, cut into 1-inch/2.5-cm cubes

2 tbsp red Thai curry paste

1¾ cups canned coconut milk

handful of fresh cilantro, chopped

1 tsp palm sugar or soft light brown sugar

1 tsp Thai fish sauce

4 oz/115 g rice noodles

3 scallions, chopped

⅔ cup fresh bean sprouts

few Thai basil leaves

1 Heat the oil in a preheated wok or large skillet over medium heat. Add the onion, garlic, and mushrooms and cook, stirring frequently, until softened but not browned.

2 Add all the fish, curry paste, and coconut milk and bring slowly to a boil. Reduce the heat and simmer for 2–3 minutes before adding half the cilantro, the sugar, and fish sauce.

3 Meanwhile, soak the noodles in a pan of boiling water according to the package directions until tender, then drain well through a metal strainer. Set the strainer with the noodles over a pan of simmering water. Add the scallions, bean sprouts, and most of the basil and steam over the noodles for 1–2 minutes or until just wilted.

4 Pile the noodles and vegetables onto warmed serving plates and top with the fish curry. Scatter the remaining cilantro and basil over the top and serve immediately.

Catalan Fish Stew

This traditional recipe takes its name, zarzuela, from the Spanish word meaning "variety show," which reflects the variety of seafood you will find in the stew. Although the fish and shellfish will vary with the day's catch, saffron, almonds, garlic, and tomatoes typically feature.

SERVES 4–6

PREP TIME 30 MINUTES

COOKING TIME 30–35 MINUTES

large pinch of saffron threads

4 tablespoons boiling water

6 tbsp olive oil

1 large onion, chopped

2 garlic cloves, finely chopped

1½ tbsp chopped fresh thyme leaves

2 bay leaves

2 red bell peppers, seeded and coarsely chopped

1 lb 12 oz/800 g canned chopped tomatoes

1 tsp smoked paprika

1 cup fish stock

scant 1 cup blanched almonds, toasted and finely ground

12–16 live mussels

12–16 live clams

1 lb 5 oz/600 g thick hake or cod fillets, skinned and cut into 2-inch/5-cm chunks

12–16 raw shrimp, shelled and deveined

salt and pepper

thick crusty bread, to serve

1 Put the saffron threads in a heatproof bowl, then add the water and set aside to infuse.

2 Meanwhile, heat the oil in a large, heavy-bottom ovenproof casserole over medium-high heat. Reduce the heat to low, then add the onion and cook, stirring occasionally, for 10 minutes, or until golden but not browned. Stir in the garlic, herbs, and red bell peppers and cook, stirring frequently, for 5 minutes, or until the peppers are softened.

3 Add the tomatoes and paprika and simmer, stirring frequently, for 5 minutes. Stir in the stock, saffron and its soaking water, and ground almonds and bring to a boil, stirring frequently. Reduce the heat and simmer for 5–10 minutes, or until the sauce reduces and thickens. Add salt and pepper to taste.

4 Meanwhile, clean the mussels and clams by scrubbing or scraping the shells and pulling out any beards that are attached to the mussels. Discard any mussels or clams with broken shells or any that refuse to close when tapped.

5 Gently stir the hake into the stew so that it doesn't break up, then add the shrimp, mussels, and clams. Reduce the heat to very low, then cover and simmer for 5 minutes, or until the hake is cooked through, the shrimp turn pink, and the mussels and clams are opened. Discard any mussels or clams that remain closed. Serve immediately with plenty of thick, crusty bread for soaking up the juices.

Shrimp and Haddock Curry

The canned red kidney beans in this mouthwatering Indian curry are a convenient, time-saving alternative to dried beans, which require a longer time to soak and cook.

SERVES 4

PREP TIME 20 MINUTES

COOKING TIME 25 MINUTES

2 tbsp vegetable oil

2 garlic cloves, chopped

4 shallots, chopped

1 tbsp grated fresh gingerroot

1 tsp mild curry powder

1 red bell pepper, seeded and chopped

7 oz/200 g canned red kidney beans, drained

3 tomatoes, chopped

3 tbsp grated fresh coconut, plus extra to garnish

3 tbsp chopped fresh cilantro

½ cup fish stock

1 lb/450 g haddock fillets, skinned

12 oz/350 g raw shrimp, shelled and deveined

5 tbsp plain yogurt

salt and pepper

to serve

boiled rice

naan bread

1 Heat the oil in a large pan over low heat. Add the garlic, shallots, ginger, and curry powder and cook, stirring, for 4 minutes, or until the shallots are slightly softened.

2 Add the red bell pepper, beans, tomatoes, coconut, and cilantro. Stir in the stock and season to taste with salt and pepper. Bring to a boil, then reduce the heat and simmer, stirring occasionally, for 15 minutes.

3 Rinse the fish fillets under cold running water, then pat dry with paper towels. Cut the fish into small chunks, then add it to the pan. Cook for 2 minutes. Add the shrimp and cook for an additional 3 minutes, or until they turn pink and the fish is cooked through—do not overcook.

4 Remove from the heat and stir in the yogurt. Arrange the fish curry on individual plates of boiled rice. Garnish with grated coconut and serve with naan bread.

Angler Fish and Mediterranean Shrimp Kabobs

The firm texture of angler fish makes it perfect for kabobs. Other firm white fish, tuna, or swordfish would be ideal alternatives. The kabobs are delicious simply served with a salad and/or rice.

SERVES 4

PREP TIME 20 MINUTES, PLUS 2–3 HOURS' MARINATING

COOKING TIME 10–15 MINUTES

1 lb 5 oz/600 g angler fish

1 green bell pepper

1 onion

3 tbsp olive oil, plus extra for oiling

3 tbsp lemon juice

2 garlic cloves, crushed

16 large raw shrimp, shelled and deveined

16 fresh bay leaves

salt and pepper

lemon wedges, to garnish

1 Cut the angler fish into 1-inch/2.5-cm chunks. Cut the green bell pepper into similar-size chunks, discarding the seeds. Cut the onion into 6 wedges, then cut each wedge in half widthwise and separate the layers.

2 For the marinade, put the oil, lemon juice, garlic, and salt and pepper to taste in a bowl and whisk together. Add the angler fish, shrimp, onion, and green bell pepper and toss together until well coated. Cover and let marinate in the refrigerator for 2–3 hours. If using wooden skewers, soak them in cold water for at least 30 minutes to prevent burning.

3 Preheat the broiler to high. Thread the pieces of fish, green bell pepper, onion, and bay leaves onto 8 oiled, flat metal or wooden kabob skewers, alternating and dividing the ingredients as evenly as possible. Arrange on an oiled broiler pan.

4 Cook the kabobs under the broiler, turning frequently and basting with any remaining marinade, for 10–15 minutes, or until cooked and lightly charred. Serve hot, garnished with lemon wedges.

Chef's tip

These kabobs are ideal for cooking over a grill and eating outdoors. Light a charcoal grill 45 minutes before starting to cook, or 10 minutes if using a gas grill, and begin cooking when the flames die down and the coals are glowing red. Cook for the same time as in the recipe.

Stir-Fried Fresh Crab with Ginger

Fresh seafood, such as the crab used in this recipe, is readily available in many parts of China. Diners enjoy sucking every last little piece of meat from the shell.

SERVES 4

PREP TIME 25 MINUTES

COOKING TIME ABOUT 12 MINUTES

3 tbsp vegetable or peanut oil

2 large fresh crabs, cleaned, broken into pieces and legs cracked with a cleaver

2 oz/55 g fresh gingerroot, julienned

3½ oz/100 g scallions, cut into 2-inch/5-cm lengths

2 tbsp light soy sauce

1 tsp sugar

pinch of white pepper

1 Heat 2 tablespoons of the oil in a preheated wok or deep pan over high heat. Add the crab and stir-fry for 3–4 minutes. Remove and set aside.

2 Heat the remaining oil in the wok or pan over high heat. Add the ginger and stir-fry until fragrant. Stir in the scallions, then the crab pieces. Add the soy sauce, sugar, and pepper, then cover and simmer for 1 minute. Serve immediately.

Chef's tip

This dish can only be made with whole fresh crabs, whether from the sea or freshwater.

Spicy Crab Tortillas

Chili, lime, cilantro, and tomatoes make wonderful companions to these tasty Mexican crab tortillas. Finish them off with generous spoonfuls of sour cream to create a truly memorable dish.

SERVES 4

PREP TIME 10 MINUTES

COOKING TIME 15 MINUTES

1 tbsp chili oil

1 large onion, coarsely chopped

2 garlic cloves, chopped

9 oz/250 g canned or freshly cooked crabmeat

1 small fresh red chili, seeded and finely chopped

2 tomatoes, chopped

1 tbsp chopped fresh cilantro, plus extra sprigs to garnish

8 small corn or flour tortillas

½ cup sour cream, plus extra to serve

lime wedges, to garnish

salt and pepper

1 Heat the oil in a skillet over medium heat. Add the onion and garlic and cook, stirring frequently, for 3–4 minutes, or until the onion is slightly softened.

2 Add the crabmeat, chili, tomatoes, and chopped cilantro. Season to taste with salt and pepper. Cook, stirring frequently, for 10 minutes. A minute before the end of the cooking time, warm the tortillas in a dry skillet for a few seconds each.

3 Remove the crab mixture from the heat. Spread a spoonful of sour cream onto each tortilla, then add some of the crab mixture and roll up. Garnish the crab tortillas with cilantro sprigs and lime wedges and serve immediately.

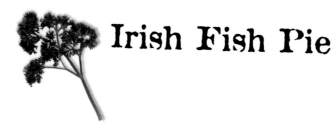

Irish Fish Pie

This unusual fish pie demonstrates that a combination of beans and cod is not only tasty, but also filling.

SERVES 4

PREP TIME 15 MINUTES

COOKING TIME 40 MINUTES

2 tbsp butter, plus extra for greasing

2 onions, chopped

2 lb 4 oz/1 kg cod fillet, skinned and cut into strips

4 rindless lean bacon slices, cut into 1¼-x-½-inch/3-x-1-cm lengths

2 tbsp chopped fresh parsley, plus extra sprigs to garnish

14 oz/400 g canned lima beans, drained and rinsed

2½ cups milk

1 lb 2 oz/500 g potatoes, very thinly sliced

salt and pepper

1 Preheat the oven to 350°F/180°C. Lightly grease an ovenproof casserole with a little butter. Arrange the onions in the bottom of the casserole and cover with the strips of cod and bacon. Sprinkle with the parsley and season to taste with salt and pepper.

2 Add the beans, then pour in the milk. Arrange the potato slices, overlapping them slightly, to cover the entire surface of the pie. Dot the potato slices with the butter.

3 Bake the pie in the oven for 40 minutes, or until the potato slices are crisp and golden. Garnish with parsley sprigs and serve immediately.

Chilies Stuffed with Fish Paste

The slight heat of the chilies beautifully complements the aromatic ginger topping in this Asian-style dish.

SERVES 4–6

PREP TIME 20 MINUTES, PLUS 20 MINUTES' MARINATING

COOKING TIME 15 MINUTES

8 oz/225 g white fish, ground

2 tbsp lightly beaten egg

4–6 fresh mild red and green chilies

vegetable or peanut oil, for pan-frying

2 garlic cloves, finely chopped

½ tsp fermented black beans, rinsed and lightly mashed

1 tbsp light soy sauce

pinch of sugar

1 tbsp water

marinade

1 tsp finely chopped fresh gingerroot

pinch of salt

pinch of white pepper

½ tsp vegetable or peanut oil

1 Combine all the ingredients for the marinade in a bowl. Add the fish, then cover and let marinate in the refrigerator for 20 minutes. Add the egg and mix by hand to form a smooth paste.

2 To prepare the chilies, cut in half lengthwise and scoop out and discard the seeds and white veins. Cut the flesh into bite-size pieces.

3 Spread each piece of chili with about ½ teaspoon of the fish paste.

4 Heat a layer of oil for pan-frying in a preheated wok or deep pan over high heat. Add the chili pieces and cook on both sides until beginning to turn golden brown. Remove with a slotted spoon, then drain on paper towels and set aside.

5 Heat 1 tablespoon of oil in the wok or deep pan over high heat. Add the garlic and stir-fry until fragrant. Stir in the beans and mix well. Stir in the soy sauce and sugar, then add the chili pieces. Add the water, then cover and simmer over low heat for 5 minutes. Serve immediately.

Chef's tip

Instead of chilies, this dish can be made with bitter melon (known as balsam pear), which should be prepared in the same way as the chilies, but blanched before being topped with the fish paste.

Moules à la Crème Normande

Mussels steamed with white wine, garlic, and parsley (moules à la marinière) are standard restaurant fare throughout France, but in Normandy, the dish is given a distinctive regional flavor with the local cider and cream.

SERVES 4–6

PREP TIME 20 MINUTES
COOKING TIME 20 MINUTES

4 lb 8 oz/2 kg live mussels
4 tbsp corn or sunflower-seed oil
2 onions, finely chopped
1 large garlic clove, finely chopped
1¾ cups cider, ideally from Normandy
1 bay leaf
generous ¾ cup heavy cream
salt and pepper
chopped fresh flat-leaf parsley, to garnish
sliced French bread, to serve

1 Clean the mussels by scrubbing or scraping the shells and pulling out any beards that are attached to them. Discard any with broken shells or any that refuse to close when tapped.

2 Heat the oil in a large, heavy-bottom pan with a tight-fitting lid over medium-high heat. Add the onions and cook, stirring frequently, for 3 minutes. Add the garlic and cook, stirring, for an additional 2 minutes, or until the onions are softened but not browned.

3 Add the cider and bay leaf and bring to a boil. Continue boiling until the cider is reduced by half.

4 Add the mussels to the pan. Reduce the heat to very low, then cover the pan tightly and simmer for 4 minutes, shaking the pan frequently, until the mussels are opened. Discard any mussels that remain closed. Transfer the remaining mussels to a large bowl, then cover and keep warm.

5 Line a large strainer with a clean piece of cheesecloth and set over a large bowl. Strain the cooking juices into the bowl, then return them to the rinsed-out pan. Add the cream, then bring to boiling point and boil until reduced by one-third.

6 Season to taste with salt and pepper, then pour over the mussels and sprinkle with parsley. Serve immediately with French bread.

Indonesian Chili Shrimp

This is a great dish for informal entertaining, as it tastes special but is very quick to prepare.

SERVES 4

PREP TIME 20 MINUTES

COOKING TIME 15 MINUTES

2 tbsp peanut or sunflower-seed oil

2 garlic cloves, finely chopped

4 shallots, finely chopped

3 fresh red chilies, seeded and thinly sliced

1-inch/2.5-cm piece fresh gingerroot or galangal, finely chopped

1 lb 2 oz/500 g large raw or cooked shrimp, shelled and deveined

⅔ cup canned coconut milk

1 tsp ground coriander

1 tbsp chopped fresh cilantro

salt

boiled rice, to serve

1 Heat the oil in a preheated wok or large, heavy-bottom skillet over medium heat. Add the garlic, shallots, chilies, and ginger and stir-fry for 4–5 minutes, or until the shallots are slightly softened. Add the raw shrimp, if using, and stir-fry for an additional 3–5 minutes, or until the shrimp have turned pink.

2 Add the coconut milk and stir in the cooked shrimp, if using, together with the ground coriander and fresh cilantro. Season to taste with salt and bring to a boil. Reduce the heat and simmer gently for 5 minutes, or until heated through.

3 Serve immediately with boiled rice.

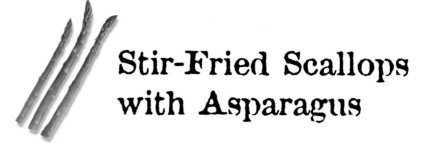

Stir-Fried Scallops with Asparagus

Fresh or frozen scallops are acceptable for this refreshing Chinese dish. Remove the shells first if you are using fresh scallops.

SERVES 4

PREP TIME 15–25 MINUTES, PLUS 20 MINUTES' STANDING

COOKING TIME 10 MINUTES

8 oz/225 g raw shucked scallops

2 tsp salt

8 oz/225 g fresh asparagus spears

3 tbsp vegetable, peanut, or sesame oil

2 oz/55 g canned bamboo shoots, drained, rinsed, and julienned, or fresh bamboo shoots, boiled in water for 30 minutes, drained, and julienned

1 small carrot, finely sliced

4 thin slices fresh gingerroot

pinch of white pepper

2 tbsp Shaoxing rice wine

2 tbsp chicken stock

1 tsp sesame oil

1 Sprinkle the scallops with half the salt. Let stand for 20 minutes.

2 Trim the asparagus, discarding the tough ends. Cut into 2-inch/5-cm pieces and blanch in a large pan of boiling water for 30 seconds. Drain and set aside.

3 Heat 1 tablespoon of the vegetable oil in a preheated wok or deep pan over high heat. Add the scallops and stir-fry for 30 seconds. Remove, then drain on paper towels and set aside.

4 Heat 1 tablespoon of the remaining vegetable oil in the wok or pan over high heat. Add the asparagus, bamboo shoots, and carrot and stir-fry for 2 minutes. Season with the remaining salt. Remove, then drain on paper towels and set aside.

5 Heat the remaining vegetable oil in the wok or pan over high heat. Add the ginger and stir-fry until fragrant. Return the scallops and vegetables to the pan and add the pepper, rice wine, and stock. Cover and simmer for 2 minutes, then toss through the sesame oil and serve immediately.

Chef's tip

The vegetables and scallops should cook for no more than 5 minutes.

Greek Pasta with Pine Nuts and Scallops

Scallops are popular in Greece. None of their flavor is lost in this quick and simple dish.

SERVES 4

PREP TIME 15 MINUTES

COOKING TIME 10–12 MINUTES

14 oz/400 g long hollow dried Greek macaroni or other short pasta

4 tbsp olive oil

1 garlic clove, finely chopped

generous ⅓ cup pine nuts

8 large raw shucked scallops, sliced

salt and pepper

2 tbsp chopped fresh basil leaves, to serve

1 Cook the macaroni in a large pan of boiling salted water for 10–12 minutes, or according to the package directions, until tender.

2 About 5 minutes before the end of the cooking time, heat the oil in a skillet over medium heat. Add the garlic and cook, stirring, for 1–2 minutes, or until softened but not browned. Add the pine nuts and cook, stirring, until browned. Add the scallops and cook, stirring constantly, until just opaque. Season to taste with salt and pepper.

3 When the pasta is cooked, drain and return to the pan. Add the scallops and all the cooking juices from the skillet to the pasta and toss together. Serve sprinkled with the basil.

Seafood Risotto

Every town in the rice-growing regions of northern Italy has its own specialty risotto, and this is Venice's.

SERVES 4

PREP TIME 25 MINUTES

COOKING TIME 45 MINUTES

8 oz/225 g live mussels with uncracked tightly closed shells (discard any that do not close when tapped)

8 oz/225 g live clams with uncracked tightly closed shells (discard any that do not close when tapped)

2 garlic cloves, halved

1 lemon, sliced

8 oz/225 g raw shrimp, shelled and deveined, wrapped in cheesecloth and tapped to release their liquid

2½ cups water

1 stick unsalted butter

1 tbsp olive oil

1 onion, finely chopped

2 tbsp chopped fresh flat-leaf parsley

generous 1½ cups risotto rice

½ cup dry white wine

225 g/8 oz cleaned raw squid, cut into small pieces, or squid rings

4 tbsp Marsala

salt and pepper

1 Clean the mussels and clams by scrubbing or scraping the shells and pulling out any beards that are attached to the mussels. Put the garlic, lemon, mussels, and clams in a large, heavy-bottom pan and add any liquid from the shrimp, reserving the shrimp. Pour in the water, then cover tightly and bring to a boil over high heat. Cook for 3–4 minutes, or until the mussels and clams are opened. Discard any that remain closed. Transfer the mussels and clams to a bowl. Strain the cooking liquid through a cheesecloth-lined strainer into a measuring cup. Make up the amount of liquid to 8 cups with water. Pour into a clean pan. Bring to a boil, then reduce the heat and simmer gently.

2 Melt 2 tbsp of the butter with the oil in a large, heavy-bottom pan over low heat. Add the onion and half the parsley and cook, stirring occasionally, for 5 minutes, or until softened. Add the rice and cook, stirring constantly, for 2–3 minutes until glistening. Add the wine and cook, stirring constantly, until almost evaporated. Add the hot cooking liquid a ladleful at a time and cook, stirring constantly, until each addition is absorbed before adding the next.

3 Meanwhile, melt 4 tbsp of the remaining butter in a heavy-bottom pan. Add the squid and cook, stirring frequently, for 3 minutes, then add the reserved (unwrapped) shrimp and cook for an additional 2–3 minutes. Stir in the Marsala, then bring to a boil and cook until all the liquid has evaporated. When the rice is tender, add the squid, shrimp, mussels, clams, and the remaining butter and parsley. Season to taste with salt and pepper. Heat through briefly and serve immediately.

Poultry and Meat

This section presents a triumph of succulent poultry and meat dishes from around the world.

Moroccan Spiced Chicken

Couscous makes a delicious and satisfying alternative to rice, and is a traditional accompaniment in many Moroccan dishes. Here it is paired beautifully with a spiced chicken and chickpea sauce.

SERVES 4

PREP TIME 15 MINUTES, PLUS 40 MINUTES' STANDING

COOKING TIME 50 MINUTES

1 eggplant, about 9 oz/250 g, thickly sliced

3 cups chicken stock

4 skinless, boneless chicken breasts, about 4 oz/115 g each

4 tbsp salted/unsalted butter

4 tbsp olive oil

1 onion, sliced

2 lb 4 oz/1 kg tomatoes

1 small fresh red chili, seeded and chopped

4 tbsp chopped fresh cilantro

1 tsp ground ginger

1 tsp ground saffron

½ tsp ground nutmeg

3 large carrots, chopped

4 zucchini, chopped

1 lb/450 g canned chickpeas

scant 1¾ cups water

12 oz/350 g couscous

salt and pepper

fresh flat-leaf parsley sprigs, to garnish

1 Sprinkle the eggplant with salt. Let stand for 30 minutes. Bring the stock to a boil in a large pan. Add the chicken, then reduce the heat and simmer gently for 20 minutes.

2 Remove the chicken with a slotted spoon and set aside. Reserve the stock. Melt half the butter with the oil in a separate large pan over medium heat. Add the onion and cook, stirring, for 3 minutes.

3 Add the tomatoes, chili, cilantro, spices, and salt and pepper to taste. Cook, stirring, for 1 minute. Rinse the eggplant and pat dry with paper towels. Cut into bite-size pieces and add to the tomato mixture with the carrots, zucchini, reserved stock, and the chickpeas with their liquid. Bring to a boil, then reduce the heat and simmer, covered, for 20 minutes.

4 Meanwhile, put the water and remaining butter into another large pan and bring to a boil. Stir in the couscous, then remove from the heat and let stand for 10 minutes. Two minutes before the end of the standing time, add the chicken to the sauce and cook for 2 minutes to heat through.

5 Pile the couscous onto individual serving plates. Lift out the chicken and arrange on the couscous, then pour over the sauce and garnish with parsley sprigs.

Indian Chili Chicken

A mixture of fresh chilies and chili powder makes this a very fiery dish, but it's also packed with aromatic flavor.

SERVES 4

PREP TIME 15 MINUTES

COOKING TIME 15–20 MINUTES

6–8 large fresh red chilies

4 tbsp corn or sunflower-seed oil

2 onions, chopped

1 tsp chili powder

1 tsp grated fresh gingerroot

2 garlic cloves, finely chopped

½ tsp cumin seeds

2 curry leaves

pinch of salt

1 lb 7 oz/650 g skinless, boneless chicken breasts, cut into cubes

2 tbsp chopped fresh cilantro

1 tbsp lime juice

4 tomatoes, cut into quarters

naan bread or boiled rice, to serve

1 Make a slit along the side of each chili. Heat the oil in a large, heavy-bottom skillet over low heat. Add the chilies and cook, turning occasionally, for 4–5 minutes, or until beginning to color. Remove with a slotted spoon and set aside.

2 Add the onions, chili powder, ginger, garlic, cumin seeds, curry leaves, and salt to the skillet and cook over medium heat, stirring, for 2–3 minutes. Add the chicken and cook, stirring frequently, for 8–10 minutes, or until tender and cooked through.

3 Stir in the cilantro and lime juice, then return the chilies to the skillet and add the tomatoes. Stir and heat briefly, then serve immediately with naan bread or boiled rice.

Thai Green Curry

You can make this fragrant dish with beef, shrimp, angler fish or, as here, chicken. Store leftover curry paste in the refrigerator.

SERVES 4

PREP TIME 25 MINUTES

COOKING TIME 15–20 MINUTES

1 lb 2 oz/500 g skinless, boneless chicken breasts

4 kaffir lime leaves

2 tbsp peanut or sunflower-seed oil

1 lemongrass stem, finely chopped

scant 1 cup canned coconut milk

16 baby eggplants, halved

2 tbsp Thai fish sauce

fresh Thai basil sprigs, to garnish

green curry paste

16 fresh green chilies

2 shallots, sliced

4 kaffir lime leaves

1 lemongrass stem, chopped

2 garlic cloves, chopped

1 tsp each of cumin and coriander seeds

1 tbsp grated fresh gingerroot or galangal

1 tsp grated lime rind

5 black peppercorns

1 tbsp sugar

salt

2 tbsp peanut or sunflower-seed oil

1 For the curry paste, seed the chilies, if liked, and coarsely chop. Put the chilies with all the remaining ingredients for the curry paste, except the oil, in a mortar and pound with a pestle. Alternatively, process in a food processor. Gradually blend in the oil.

2 Cut the chicken into cubes. Coarsely tear 2 lime leaves and cut the other 2 lime leaves into thin strips.

3 Heat the oil in a preheated wok or large, heavy-bottom skillet over medium-high heat. Add 2 tablespoons of the curry paste and stir-fry briefly until fragrant.

4 Add the chicken, torn lime leaves, and lemongrass and stir-fry for 3–4 minutes, or until the meat begins to color. Add the coconut milk and eggplants and simmer gently for 8–10 minutes, or until the eggplants are tender and the chicken is cooked through.

5 Stir in the fish sauce and serve immediately, garnished with basil sprigs and the lime leaf strips.

Yakitori Chicken

These succulent chicken kabobs from Japan are accompanied by a deliciously sweet sauce flavored with mirin and saki. They make elegant fare for dinner parties and entertaining.

MAKES 6 SKEWERS

PREP TIME 10 MINUTES, PLUS 30 MINUTES' SOAKING/COOLING

COOKING TIME ABOUT 12 MINUTES

6 tbsp soy sauce

6 tbsp mirin

4 tbsp sake

2 tbsp superfine sugar

4 skinless, boneless chicken thighs or 2 chicken breasts, about 14 oz/400 g total weight, cut into 24 chunks

4 scallions, cut into 18 short lengths, plus extra to garnish

1 If using wooden skewers, soak them in cold water for at least 30 minutes to prevent burning.

2 Meanwhile, put the soy sauce, mirin, sake, and sugar in a small pan and bring to a boil. Reduce the heat and simmer for 1 minute, then remove from the heat and let cool. Separate out a little of the mixture for drizzling over the skewers.

3 Preheat the broiler to high. Thread 4 pieces of chicken and 3 pieces of scallion onto each skewer, then brush the skewers with the soy sauce mixture. Cook under the broiler for 4 minutes, then turn over and brush with more of the soy sauce mixture. Cook for an additional 4 minutes, or until the chicken is tender and cooked through.

4 Serve the skewers drizzled with the reserved soy sauce mixture, garnished with scallions.

Greek Chicken Kabobs with Yogurt Sauce

Kabobs, small cubes of meat grilled on a spit or skewer, have been popular in Greece since ancient times. Lamb is the usual choice, but this recipe uses chicken, which is marinated in, and then served with, a traditional, tenderizing yogurt sauce.

SERVES 4

PREP TIME 20 MINUTES, PLUS 1 HOUR'S MARINATING/SOAKING

COOKING TIME 15 MINUTES

4 large skinless, boneless chicken breasts, about 5 oz/140 g each

olive oil, for oiling

8 firm fresh rosemary stems (optional)

shredded romaine lettuce, to serve

lemon wedges, to garnish

yogurt sauce

1¼ cups strained plain yogurt

2 garlic cloves, crushed

juice of ½ lemon

1 tbsp chopped fresh herbs, such as oregano, dill, tarragon, or parsley

salt and pepper

1 For the sauce, put the yogurt, garlic, lemon juice, herbs, and salt and pepper to taste in a large, nonmetallic bowl and mix well together. Set aside a quarter of the sauce, then cover and refrigerate until required.

2 Cut the chicken into chunks measuring about 1½ inches/4 cm square. Add to the remaining sauce in the bowl and toss until the chicken pieces are well coated. Cover and let marinate in the refrigerator for about 1 hour. Meanwhile, if you are using wooden skewers, soak them in cold water for at least 30 minutes.

3 Preheat the broiler to medium-high. Thread the pieces of chicken onto 8 oiled, flat metal skewers, wooden skewers, or rosemary stems and arrange on an oiled broiler pan.

4 Cook the kabobs under the broiler, turning and basting occasionally with the remaining marinade in the bowl, for 15 minutes, or until lightly browned and tender.

5 Five minutes before the end of cooking time, pour the reserved yogurt sauce into a pan and heat gently, but do not boil. Serve the kabobs on a bed of shredded lettuce and garnish with lemon wedges. Accompany with the yogurt sauce.

Coq au Vin

Traditional recipes often yield wonderfully tasty results, and this dish is no exception. Serve this perennial French favorite with warm crusty bread or garlic bread to mop up the delicious wine-flavored juices.

SERVES 4

PREP TIME 20 MINUTES

COOKING TIME 1¼ HOURS

4 tbsp salted/unsalted butter

2 tbsp olive oil

4 lb/1.8 kg chicken pieces

4 oz/115 g rindless smoked bacon slices, cut into strips

4 oz/115 g baby onions

4 oz/115 g cremini mushrooms, halved

2 garlic cloves, finely chopped

2 tbsp brandy

scant 1 cup red wine

1¼ cups chicken stock

1 bouquet garni

2 tbsp all-purpose flour

salt and pepper

bay leaves, to garnish

1 Melt half the butter with the oil in a large, ovenproof casserole. Add the chicken and cook over medium heat, stirring, for 8–10 minutes, or until golden brown all over. Add the bacon, onions, mushrooms, and garlic.

2 Pour in the brandy and set it alight with a match or taper. When the flames have died down, add the wine, stock, and bouquet garni and season to taste with salt and pepper. Bring to a boil, then reduce the heat and simmer gently, covered, for 1 hour, or until the chicken pieces are tender and the juices run clear when a skewer is inserted into the thickest part of the meat. Meanwhile, make a beurre manié by mashing the remaining butter with the flour in a small bowl.

3 Remove and discard the bouquet garni. Transfer the chicken to a large plate and keep warm. Stir the beurre manié into the casserole, a little at a time. Bring to a boil, then return the chicken to the casserole and serve immediately, garnished with bay leaves.

Chef's tip

You can cook the chicken in the oven instead of on the stove. Preheat the oven to 325°F/160°C, and cover and transfer the casserole to the oven once the mixture has come to a boil in Step 2. Cook for 1 hour, then follow Step 3.

Chicken and Chili Enchiladas

In this popular Mexican recipe corn tortillas are wrapped around a spicy filling and baked in a tasty sauce for a substantial meal.

SERVES 4

PREP TIME 20 MINUTES

COOKING TIME 35 MINUTES

corn oil, for oiling

5 fresh hot green chilies, such as jalapeño or serrano, seeded and chopped

1 Spanish onion, chopped

2 garlic cloves, chopped

2 tbsp chopped fresh cilantro

2 tbsp lime juice

½ cup chicken stock

2 beefsteak tomatoes, peeled, seeded, and chopped

pinch of sugar

12 oz/350 g cooked chicken, shredded

3 oz/85 g queso anejo or Cheddar cheese, grated

2 tsp chopped fresh oregano

8 corn or flour tortillas

salt

1 Preheat the oven to 350°F/180°C. Oil a large ovenproof dish. For the sauce, put two-thirds of the chilies, the onion, garlic, cilantro, lime juice, stock, tomatoes, and sugar in a food processor and pulse until well blended. Scrape into a pan and simmer over medium heat for 10 minutes, or until thickened.

2 Mix the remaining chilies, the chicken, ½ cup of the cheese, and the oregano together in a bowl. Season to taste with salt and stir in half the sauce.

3 Heat the tortillas in a dry, heavy-bottom skillet or in the microwave according to the package directions. Divide the chicken mixture between the tortillas, spooning it down the centers, then roll up and arrange, seam-side down, in the ovenproof dish.

4 Pour the remaining sauce over the enchiladas and sprinkle with the remaining cheese. Bake in the oven for 20 minutes. Serve immediately.

Spanish-Style Chicken with Onions and Ham

Marinating chicken breasts in lemon juice is an old trick for tenderizing the flesh. For best results, leave the chicken in the marinade overnight.

SERVES 4

PREP TIME 10 MINUTES, PLUS 8 HOURS' MARINATING

COOKING TIME 40 MINUTES

4 skin-on, boneless chicken breasts, about 4½ oz/125 g each

⅔ cup freshly squeezed lemon juice (3–4 lemons)

1–1½ tsp mild or hot Spanish paprika, to taste

about 2 tbsp olive oil

2½ oz/70 g serrano ham, diced

4 large onions, thinly sliced

½ cup dry white wine

½ cup chicken stock

salt and pepper

fresh thyme sprigs, to garnish

1 Put the chicken breasts in a nonmetallic bowl. Pour over the lemon juice, then cover and let marinate in the refrigerator overnight.

2 Remove the chicken from the marinade and pat dry with paper towels. Rub the skins with the paprika and salt and pepper to taste.

3 Heat 2 tablespoons of oil in a large, heavy-bottom skillet with a tight-fitting lid over medium-high heat. Add the chicken breasts, skin-side down, and cook for 5 minutes, or until the skins are crisp and golden. Remove with a slotted spoon and set aside.

4 Stir the ham into the fat remaining in the skillet, then cover and cook for 2 minutes, or until the fat renders. Add the onions and cook, stirring occasionally and adding a little extra oil if necessary, for 5 minutes, or until softened but not browned.

5 Add the wine and stock and bring to a boil, stirring. Return the chicken to the skillet and season to taste with salt and pepper. Reduce the heat, then cover and simmer for 20 minutes, or until the chicken is tender and the juices run clear when a skewer is inserted into the thickest part of the meat. Transfer to a plate and keep warm.

6 Bring the sauce to a boil and bubble until the cooking juices reduce. Taste and adjust the seasoning. Divide the onion mixture between 4 warmed plates and arrange a chicken breast on top of each. Garnish with thyme sprigs and serve immediately.

Chicken Gumbo

A cross between a soup and a stew, gumbo is one of the great dishes of Louisiana Creole cooking. All gumbos begin with the essential slowly cooked roux, and are then thickened with okra or filé powder.

SERVES 4–6

PREP TIME 20 MINUTES

COOKING TIME 2¼ HOURS

1 chicken, about 3 lb 5 oz/1.5 kg, cut into 6 pieces

2 celery stalks, 1 broken in half and 1 finely chopped

1 carrot, chopped

2 onions, 1 sliced and 1 chopped

2 bay leaves

4 tbsp corn or peanut oil

⅓ cup all-purpose flour

2 large garlic cloves, crushed

1 green bell pepper, seeded and diced

1 lb/450 g fresh okra, trimmed, then cut crosswise into ½-inch/1-cm slices

8 oz/225 g andouille sausage or Polish kielbasa, sliced

2 tbsp tomato paste

1 tsp dried thyme

½ tsp cayenne pepper

14 oz/400 g canned peeled plum tomatoes

salt and pepper

boiled rice, to serve

1 Put the chicken in a large pan, then cover with water and bring to a boil over medium-high heat, skimming off any foam that appears on the surface. When the foam stops rising, reduce the heat to medium, then add the celery stalk halves, carrot, sliced onion, 1 bay leaf, and ¼ teaspoon of salt and simmer for 20 minutes, or until the chicken is tender and the juices run clear when a skewer is inserted into the thickest part of the meat. Strain the chicken, reserving 4 cups of the liquid. When the chicken is cool enough to handle, remove and discard the skin, bones, and flavorings. Cut the flesh into bite-size pieces and set aside.

2 Heat the oil in a large pan over medium-high heat. Reduce the heat to low, then sprinkle in the flour and stir to make the roux. Stir constantly for 30 minutes, or until the roux turns hazelnut brown. If black specks appear, it is burnt and you will have to start again.

3 Add the chopped celery, chopped onion, garlic, bell pepper, and okra. Increase the heat to medium-high and cook, stirring frequently, for 5 minutes. Add the sausage and cook, stirring frequently, for 2 minutes.

4 Stir in the remaining ingredients, including the bay leaf, reserved cooking liquid and half a teaspoon salt. Bring to a boil, crushing the tomatoes with a wooden spoon. Reduce the heat and simmer uncovered for 30 minutes. Add the chicken and simmer for 30 minutes. Season if necessary and spoon the gumbo over the rice.

Hainan Chicken Rice

This dish is originally from the semitropical Hainan Island in the south of China, but was introduced by migrants to Singapore, where it is now almost a national dish.

SERVES 4–6

PREP TIME 20 MINUTES

COOKING TIME 1–1¼ HOURS

1 chicken, about 3 lb 5 oz/1.5 kg

2 oz/55 g fresh young gingerroot, crushed

2 garlic cloves, crushed

1 scallion, tied in a knot

1 tsp salt

2 tbsp vegetable or peanut oil

chili or soy dipping sauce, to serve

rice

2 tbsp vegetable or peanut oil

5 garlic cloves, finely chopped

5 shallots, finely chopped

generous 1½ cups long-grain rice

3¾ cups chicken stock

1 tsp salt

1 Wash the chicken and dry thoroughly. Stuff the body cavity with the ginger, garlic, scallion, and salt.

2 Fill a large pan with water and bring to the boil. Put the chicken, breast-side down, into the pan, then return the water to a boil. Reduce the heat and simmer, covered, turning the chicken over once, for 30–40 minutes, or until tender and the juices run clear when a skewer is inserted into the thickest part of the meat.

3 Remove the chicken and rinse under running cold water for 2 minutes to prevent any additional cooking. Drain, then rub the oil into the skin. Set aside.

4 To prepare the rice, heat the oil in a preheated wok or deep pan over high heat. Add the garlic and shallots and stir-fry until fragrant. Add the rice and vigorously stir-fry for 3 minutes. Add the stock and salt. Bring to a boil, then reduce the heat and simmer, covered, for 20 minutes. Turn off the heat and let the rice steam for an additional 5–10 minutes, or until the rice grains are tender.

5 To serve, chop the chicken horizontally, through the bone and skin, into chunky wedges. Serve with the rice and dipping sauce.

Sweet-and-Sour Chicken

The Chinese usually associate a sweet-and-sour sauce with fish rather than meat, and would prepare the sauce in a very different way. But this rendering is particularly popular in the West.

SERVES 4–6

PREP TIME 15 MINUTES, PLUS 20 MINUTES' MARINATING

COOKING TIME 15 MINUTES

1 lb/450 g skinless, boneless chicken, cubed

5 tbsp vegetable or peanut oil

½ tsp crushed garlic

½ tsp finely chopped fresh gingerroot

1 green bell pepper, coarsely chopped

1 onion, coarsely chopped

1 carrot, finely sliced

1 tsp sesame oil

1 tbsp finely chopped scallion

marinade

2 tsp light soy sauce

1 tsp Shaoxing rice wine

pinch of white pepper

½ tsp salt

dash of sesame oil

sauce

8 tbsp rice vinegar

4 tbsp sugar

2 tsp light soy sauce

6 tbsp tomato ketchup

1 Put all the ingredients for the marinade in a bowl, then add the chicken and turn to coat well. Cover and let marinate in the refrigerator for at least 20 minutes.

2 For the sauce, heat the vinegar in a pan and add the sugar, soy sauce, and tomato ketchup. Stir to dissolve the sugar, then remove from the heat and set aside.

3 Heat 3 tablespoons of the vegetable oil in a preheated wok or deep pan over high heat. Remove the chicken from the marinade, then add to the pan and stir-fry until beginning to turn golden brown. Remove with a slotted spoon and set aside.

4 Heat the remaining vegetable oil in the wok or pan over high heat. Add the garlic and ginger and stir-fry until fragrant. Add the vegetables and stir-fry for 2 minutes. Return the chicken to the pan and stir-fry for 1 minute. Add the sauce and sesame oil, then stir in the scallion. Serve immediately.

Chef's tip

Vary the amounts of vinegar and tomato ketchup in the sauce for a stronger or lighter sweet–sour finish.

Mongolian Fire Pot

The traditional Mongolian fire pot used for this dish is a ring-shaped vessel. It fits over a chimney that holds burning charcoal, which heats the water in which the foods are cooked. If you don't have a fire pot, you can use a heavy-bottom pan or ovenproof casserole set on a hot plate.

SERVES 6

PREP TIME 25 MINUTES, PLUS 20 MINUTES' SOAKING

COOKING TIME 2–5 MINUTES PER INGREDIENT

2½ cups chicken stock

6 dried Chinese mushrooms, soaked in warm water for 20 minutes

1 lb/450 g lean rib-eye or sirloin steak, very finely sliced

1 lb/450 g lean chicken, very finely sliced

8 oz/225 g raw shrimp, shelled and deveined

5½ oz/150 g canned bamboo shoots, drained, rinsed, and julienned, or fresh bamboo shoots, boiled in water for 30 minutes, drained, and julienned

1½ cups snow peas

1 lb/450 g Napa cabbage, chopped

chili and soy dipping sauces

2 tsp salt

8 oz/225 g bean thread noodles

1 Pour the stock into the fire pot. Drain the mushrooms, squeezing out any excess water, and finely slice, discarding any tough stems. Add to the stock.

2 Arrange the meat, shrimp, and vegetables on a platter. Put the dipping sauces in small individual dishes. Bring the stock to a boil in the pot and add the salt. Throw in a few noodles and vegetables.

3 To eat, the diners each cook their own food by holding it in the stock with their chopsticks until cooked through, then dip it in their choice of dipping sauces. When the last foods have been cooked, the cooking liquid is served in individual bowls.

Chef's tip

The fun of this dish is that everyone cooks their own food around the central pot, and the water transforms itself into a delicious broth that can be eaten last.

Coconut Beef Curry

This is a warm and satisfying beef curry infused with the rich, exciting flavors of Thailand. All it needs by way of accompaniment is a generous serving of freshly cooked rice.

SERVES 4

PREP TIME 20 MINUTES, PLUS 45 MINUTES' SOAKING

COOKING TIME 35–45 MINUTES

1 tbsp each of ground coriander and ground cumin

⅔ cup water

2¾ oz/75 g creamed coconut

1 lb/450 g beef tenderloin, cut into strips

1¾ cups coconut milk

⅓ cup unsalted peanuts, finely chopped

2 tbsp Thai fish sauce

1 tsp palm sugar or soft light brown sugar

4 kaffir lime leaves

boiled rice with chopped fresh cilantro, to serve

mussaman curry paste

4 large dried red chilies

2 tsp shrimp paste

3 shallots, finely chopped

3 garlic cloves, finely chopped

1-inch/2.5-cm piece fresh galangal, finely chopped

2 lemongrass stems, finely chopped

2 cloves

1 tbsp each of coriander and cumin seeds

seeds from 3 green cardamom pods

1 tsp each of black peppercorns and salt

1 For the curry paste, cut off and discard the chili stems and put the chilies in a bowl. Cover with hot water and set aside to soak for 45 minutes. Wrap the shrimp paste in foil and broil or dry-fry in a skillet for 2–3 minutes, turning once or twice. Remove from the broiler or skillet. Dry-fry the shallots, garlic, galangal, lemongrass, cloves and coriander, cumin, and cardamom seeds over low heat, stirring frequently, for 3–4 minutes, or until lightly browned. Transfer to a food processor and process until finely ground. Add the chilies and their soaking water, peppercorns, and salt and process again. Add the shrimp paste and process again to a smooth paste.

2 Combine the ground coriander and cumin and 3 tablespoons of the curry paste in a bowl. Pour the water into a pan, then add the creamed coconut and heat until it has dissolved. Add the curry paste mixture and simmer for 1 minute.

3 Add the beef and simmer for 6–8 minutes, then add the coconut milk, peanuts, fish sauce, and sugar. Simmer gently for 15–20 minutes, or until the meat is tender.

4 Add the lime leaves and simmer for 1–2 minutes. Serve the curry hot, with boiled rice with chopped fresh cilantro stirred through it.

Chef's tip

The remaining curry paste can be stored in an airtight container in the refrigerator for up to 3 weeks.

Tenderloin Steak with Bleu Cheese Sauce

This North American specialty is a decadent dish for lovers of bleu cheese. Individual sirloin or rump steaks can be used as an alternative to the whole tenderloin when serving as a family meal.

SERVES 6

PREP TIME 20 MINUTES

COOKING TIME 20–30 MINUTES

1 beef tenderloin, about 3 lb/1.3 kg

5 tbsp salted/unsalted butter

olive or vegetable oil, for oiling

4½ oz/125 g bleu cheese, such as Gorgonzola, Roquefort, Stilton, or Danish Bleu, crumbled

1 shallot, finely chopped

scant ½ cup Madeira or dry sherry

⅔ cup heavy cream

salt and pepper

chopped fresh parsley, to garnish

green beans, to serve

1 Preheat the broiler or gas grill to high, or light grill coals. Tie the tenderloin widthwise at regular intervals with string to form a neat shape. Put the butter in a small bowl and beat with a wooden spoon until softened. Spread 2 tablespoons of the softened butter evenly all over the steak. Season to taste with pepper.

2 Put the tenderloin onto an oiled broiler rack or grill grid and cook under or over high heat, turning frequently, until browned on all sides, then cook over medium heat for 18–25 minutes until cooked according to your taste, turning frequently.

3 Meanwhile, add the bleu cheese to the remaining softened butter and blend together until the mixture is smooth.

4 Put the shallot and Madeira into a pan, then bring to a boil and boil until reduced to about 2 tablespoons. Stir in the cream, then let simmer for 3 minutes. Add the cheese mixture, a little at a time, whisking after each addition until the sauce is smooth. When all the cheese mixture has been added, remove from the heat. Season to taste with salt and pepper.

5 Transfer the cooked tenderloin to a warmed serving dish and let rest for 5 minutes. Slice the tenderloin into steaks and serve with green beans and the bleu cheese sauce drizzled over, garnished with chopped parsley. Serve any remaining sauce separately in a pitcher.

Cilantro Lamb Kabobs

In any bazaar or market in a northern Indian city, street vendors will cook these subtly spiced kabobs to order. They are cooked in a tandoor (clay oven) to produce a dry exterior that keeps the center tender; using a hot preheated broiler or cooking over glowing coals also gives good results.

MAKES 4–6 SKEWERS

PREP TIME 20 MINUTES, PLUS 45 MINUTES' STANDING

COOKING TIME 5–7 MINUTES

1 lb 9 oz/700 g fresh ground lamb

1 onion, grated

3 tbsp finely chopped fresh cilantro leaves and stems, plus extra sprigs to garnish

3 tbsp finely chopped fresh mint

3 tbsp gram flour

1½ tbsp ground almonds

1-inch/2.5-cm piece fresh gingerroot, grated

3 tbsp lemon juice

2 tbsp plain yogurt

2 tsp ground cumin

2 tsp ground coriander

1½ tsp salt

1½ tsp garam masala

1 tsp ground cinnamon

pepper

to serve

lemon wedges

mixed salad

1 Put all the ingredients in a large bowl and use your hands to incorporate everything until the texture is smooth. Cover with a clean dish towel and let stand for 45 minutes at room temperature. If using wooden kabob skewers, soak in cold water for at least 30 minutes to prevent burning.

2 With wet hands, divide the lamb mixture into 24 balls. Working with one ball at a time, mold it around a long, flat metal or wooden skewer, shaping it into a cylinder shape. Continue until all the mixture has been used and you have filled 4–6 skewers.

3 Preheat the broiler or gas grill to its highest setting, or light grill coals and let them burn until they turn gray. Put the skewers onto an oiled broiler rack or grill grid and cook for 5–7 minutes, turning frequently, until the lamb is completely cooked through and not at all pink when you pierce it with the point of a knife. Serve garnished with cilantro sprigs and with lemon wedges for squeezing over and a mixed salad.

Chef's tip

If you don't want to be bothered shaping the lamb mixture into skewers, form 6 patties. Broil as above, but increase the cooking time to 4 minutes on each side.

Shepherds Pie

Traditionally, this British classic was put together from leftover lamb from the Sunday joint and served as a family meal in the week. Using good-quality ground lamb gives a much better flavor. Shepherds pie is often confused with cottage pie, but that is always made with ground beef.

SERVES 6

PREP TIME 15 MINUTES

COOKING TIME 1½ HOURS

1 tbsp olive oil

2 onions, finely chopped

2 garlic cloves, finely chopped

1 lb 8 oz/675 g good-quality fresh ground lamb

2 carrots, finely chopped

1 tbsp all-purpose flour

scant 1 cup beef or chicken stock

½ cup red wine

Worcestershire sauce (optional)

salt and pepper

creamed potato

1 lb 8 oz/675 g mealy potatoes, such as Russet or Yukon, peeled and cut into chunks

4 tbsp butter

2 tbsp cream or milk

salt and pepper

1 Preheat the oven to 350°F/180°C.

2 Heat the oil in a large ovenproof casserole over medium heat. Add the onions and cook, stirring frequently, for 5 minutes, or until softened but not browned. Add the garlic and stir well.

3 Increase the heat and add the ground lamb. Cook quickly to brown the meat all over, stirring constantly to break up the meat. Add the carrots and season well with salt and pepper. Stir in the flour and add the stock and wine. Stir well and heat until simmering and thickened.

4 Cover and cook in the oven for 1 hour. Check the consistency from time to time and add a little more stock or wine, if necessary. The meat mixture should be quite thick, but not dry. Season to taste with salt and pepper and add a little Worcestershire sauce, if liked.

5 Meanwhile, cook the potatoes in a large pan of boiling salted water for 15–20 minutes. Drain well and mash with a potato masher until smooth. Add the butter and cream and season well with salt and pepper. Spoon the lamb mixture into an ovenproof serving dish and spread or pipe the creamed potato on top.

6 Increase the oven temperature to 400°F/200°C and cook the pie for 15–20 minutes at the top of the oven until golden brown. You might like to finish it off under a preheated medium broiler for a really crisp, brown topping to the potato.

Pork and Vegetables in Black Bean Sauce

Black bean sauce is a traditional Chinese blend of soybeans and special spices. Its unique aroma complements both meat and vegetables, making a rich and robust sauce that is great for steaming and stir-frying.

SERVES 4

PREP TIME 15 MINUTES

COOKING TIME 10–15 MINUTES

8 tbsp vegetable or peanut oil

4 oz/115 g rice vermicelli noodles

4 belly pork (side pork) strips, thickly sliced

1 red onion, sliced

2 garlic cloves, chopped

1-inch/2.5-cm piece fresh gingerroot, thinly sliced

1 large fresh red chili, seeded and chopped

4 oz/115 g baby corn, halved lengthwise

1 red bell pepper, seeded and sliced

6 oz/175 g broccoli, cut into florets

5½-oz/150-g jar black bean sauce

⅔ cup fresh bean sprouts

1 Heat the oil in a preheated wok or large skillet over high heat. Add the rice noodles, in batches, and cook for 30 seconds, or until crisp and puffed up. Remove with tongs, then drain on paper towels and set aside. Discard all but 2 tablespoons of the oil.

2 Add the pork, onion, garlic, ginger, and chili to the wok or skillet and stir-fry for 4–5 minutes, or until the meat is well browned all over.

3 Add the baby corn, red bell pepper, and broccoli and stir-fry for 3–4 minutes, or until the vegetables are just tender. Stir in the black bean sauce and bean sprouts and cook, stirring, for an additional 2–3 minutes. Serve immediately, topped with the crispy noodles.

Japanese Sweet Roast Pork

The Japanese are masters of the art of graceful food presentation, and this sweet roast pork dish not only lives up to that reputation, it tastes as good as it looks.

SERVES 4

PREP TIME 10 MINUTES, PLUS 2 HOURS' MARINATING

COOKING TIME 1 HOUR 35 MINUTES

1 lb 10 oz/750 g boneless belly of pork (side pork), in one piece, rind and most of the fat removed

1 garlic clove, crushed

1 tbsp vegetable oil

salt

cress, to garnish

chopped cucumber, to serve

marinade

8 tbsp shoyu (Japanese soy sauce), plus extra to serve

4 tbsp sake

5 tbsp mirin

3 tbsp brown sugar

1 Preheat the oven to 400°F/200°C.

2 Rub the pork with the garlic and salt to taste. Heat the oil in a large skillet over high heat. Add the pork and brown all over.

3 Transfer the pork to a baking sheet and roast in the oven for 1½ hours, or until the pork is tender.

4 Meanwhile, mix all the ingredients for the marinade together in a bowl. Rinse the pork in hot water and shake off any excess. Lay the pork in a dish and pour over the marinade. Cover with plastic wrap and let marinate in the refrigerator for at least 2 hours.

5 Remove the pork from the marinade and thinly slice to serve. Serve with extra shoyu and garnished with cress and chopped cucumber.

Pork Ribs Braised in Soy Sauce

Aromatic, sticky, and delicious, this finger-licking Chinese dish is a favorite across generations.

SERVES 4

PREP TIME 10 MINUTES, PLUS 20 MINUTES' MARINATING

COOKING TIME 1 HOUR 35 MINUTES–1 HOUR 50 MINUTES

1 lb 5 oz/600 g pork ribs, cut into bite-size pieces

1 tbsp dark soy sauce

1 whole garlic head

2 tbsp vegetable or peanut oil or shortening

1 cinnamon stick

2 star anise

3 tbsp light soy sauce

2 oz/55 g rock sugar

¾ cup water

1 Put the pork ribs in a shallow dish and sprinkle over the dark soy sauce. Cover and let marinate in the refrigerator for at least 20 minutes.

2 Break the garlic head into cloves, leaving the individual skins intact.

3 Heat the oil in a preheated wok or deep pan over high heat. Add the garlic cloves and stir-fry for 1 minute. Toss in the cinnamon and star anise and stir-fry for 1 minute. Add the pork and stir-fry until beginning to brown, then stir in the light soy sauce, sugar, and water and cook, stirring, until the sugar has dissolved. Simmer gently, uncovered, for 30 minutes, stirring frequently.

4 Cover and simmer for 1–1¼ hours, or until the meat is very tender and the gravy thick and concentrated.

Chef's tip

A nice option is to add halved hard-cooked eggs just before the dish has finished cooking.

Vegetables, Salads, and Accompaniments

Whoever said vegetables had to be dull? These impressive dishes will be a success whatever the occasion.

Imam Bayildi

The name of this dish means "the Imam fainted." A Muslim holy man was said to have been so overjoyed by its aroma that he swooned with delight. It is suitable for vegetarians and vegans.

SERVES 4

PREP TIME 15 MINUTES, PLUS 2 HOURS' STANDING, COOLING, AND CHILLING

COOKING TIME 45 MINUTES

2 eggplants
4 tbsp olive oil
2 onions, thinly sliced
2 garlic cloves, finely chopped
1 green bell pepper, seeded and sliced
14 oz/400 g canned chopped tomatoes
3 tbsp sugar
1 tsp ground coriander
2 tbsp chopped fresh cilantro
salt and pepper

1 Preheat the oven to 375°F/190°C. Halve the eggplants lengthwise, then slash the flesh 4 or 5 times and sprinkle generously with salt. Put in a colander and let stand for 30 minutes. Rinse and pat dry with paper towels.

2 Heat the oil in a large, heavy-bottom skillet over medium heat. Add the eggplants, cut-side down, and cook for 5 minutes. Remove with a slotted spoon, then drain well on paper towels and transfer to a casserole. Add the onions, garlic, and green bell pepper to the skillet and cook, stirring occasionally, for 10 minutes. Add the tomatoes, sugar, and ground coriander and season to taste with salt and pepper. Stir in the fresh cilantro.

3 Spoon the onion and tomato mixture on top of the eggplant halves, then cover and bake in the oven for 30 minutes. Remove from the oven and let cool. Cover and chill in the refrigerator for 1 hour before serving.

Chef's tip

Even after salting, eggplants tend to absorb a lot of oil, so you may need to add a little more before cooking the onions in Step 2.

Nachos

Who can resist diving into a molten mountain of nachos and biting into that great combination of the soggy, chewy, and crispy? This Mexican dish is very easy to prepare, especially if you use canned refried beans, and they are delicious with an icy glass of tequila.

SERVES 6

PREP TIME 10 MINUTES

COOKING TIME 5–8 MINUTES

6 oz/175 g tortilla chips

14 oz/400 g canned refried beans, warmed

2 tbsp finely chopped bottled jalapeño chilies

7 oz/200 g canned or bottled pimientos or roasted bell peppers, drained and finely sliced

1 cup grated Gruyère cheese

1 cup grated Cheddar cheese

salt and pepper

to serve

guacamole

sour cream

1 Preheat the oven to 400°F/200°C.

2 Spread the tortilla chips out over the bottom of a large, shallow ovenproof dish or roasting pan. Cover with the refried beans. Sprinkle over the chilies and pimientos and season to taste with salt and pepper. Mix the cheeses together in a bowl and sprinkle on top.

3 Bake in the oven for 5–8 minutes, or until the cheese is bubbling and melted. Serve immediately with some guacamole and sour cream.

Crisp Noodle and Vegetable Stir-Fry

The Chinese carefully select vegetables to achieve a harmonious balance of contrasting colors and textures. Once you have chopped the vegetables, this dish is quick and easy to put together, and makes an attractive and nutritious meal.

SERVES 4

PREP TIME 20 MINUTES

COOKING TIME 10 MINUTES

peanut or sunflower-seed oil, for deep-frying

4 oz/115 g rice vermicelli noodles, broken into 3-inch/7.5-cm lengths

¾ cup green beans, cut into short lengths

2 carrots, cut into thin sticks

2 zucchini, cut into thin sticks

4 oz/115 g shiitake mushrooms, sliced

1-inch/2.5-cm piece fresh gingerroot, shredded

½ small head Napa cabbage, shredded

4 scallions, shredded

generous ½ cup fresh bean sprouts

2 tbsp dark soy sauce

2 tbsp rice wine

large pinch of sugar

2 tbsp coarsely chopped fresh cilantro

1 Half-fill a preheated wok or deep, heavy-bottom skillet with oil. Heat to 350–375°F/180–190°C, or until a cube of bread browns in 30 seconds.

2 Add the noodles, in batches, and cook for 30 seconds, or until crisp and puffed up. Remove with tongs, then drain on paper towels and set aside. Pour off all but 2 tablespoons of oil from the wok.

3 Heat the remaining oil in the wok over high heat. Add the green beans and stir-fry for 2 minutes.

4 Add the carrot and zucchini sticks, mushrooms, and ginger and stir-fry for an additional 2 minutes.

5 Add the Napa cabbage, scallions, and bean sprouts and stir-fry for an additional minute.

6 Add the soy sauce, rice wine, and sugar and cook, stirring constantly, for 1 minute.

7 Add the noodles and cilantro and toss well. Serve immediately.

Chef's tip

This dish also looks attractive if you serve the noodles in a small nest on top of the stir-fried vegetables, rather than tossing them with the vegetables in Step 7.

Chili-Yogurt Mushrooms

If you consider mushrooms to be uninteresting, think again. In this classic Indian treatment, they are aromatically spiced and enriched with a creamy yogurt sauce. The recipe uses cremini mushrooms, but white mushrooms can be used instead.

Serves 4–6

Prep Time 10 minutes

Cooking Time about 20 minutes

4 tbsp ghee or 4 tbsp vegetable or peanut oil

2 large onions, chopped

4 large garlic cloves, crushed

14 oz/400 g canned chopped tomatoes

1 tsp ground turmeric

1 tsp garam masala

½ tsp chili powder

1 lb 10 oz/750 g cremini mushrooms, thickly sliced

pinch of sugar

½ cup plain yogurt

salt

chopped fresh cilantro and cilantro sprigs, to garnish

1 Melt the ghee in a kadhai, wok, or large skillet over medium-high heat. Add the onions and cook, stirring frequently, for 5–8 minutes, or until golden. Add the garlic and cook, stirring, for an additional 2 minutes.

2 Add the tomatoes and their juice and stir well. Add the turmeric, garam masala, and chili powder and cook, stirring, for 3 minutes.

3 Add the mushrooms, sugar, and salt to taste and cook, stirring occasionally, for 8 minutes, or until the mushrooms have given off their liquid and are tender.

4 Remove from the heat, then stir in the yogurt, a little at a time, beating vigorously to prevent it curdling. Taste and adjust the seasoning, if necessary. Garnish with cilantro and serve immediately.

Chef's tip

Adding the salt with the mushrooms in Step 3 draws out their moisture, giving extra flavor to the juices.

Spinach and Mushroom Chimichangas

These crisp deep-fried Mexican pockets are universally appealing and are quick to make. Enjoy this feast with a tequila.

SERVES 4

PREP TIME 20 MINUTES

COOKING TIME 35 MINUTES

2 tbsp olive oil

1 large onion, finely chopped

8 oz/225 g small mushrooms, finely sliced

2 fresh mild green chilies, seeded and finely chopped

2 garlic cloves, finely chopped

9 oz/250 g spinach leaves, torn into pieces if large

1½ cups grated Cheddar cheese

8 corn or flour tortillas

vegetable oil, for deep-frying

to serve

guacamole

sour cream

seeded and chopped tomatoes

chopped onions

1 Heat the olive oil in a large, heavy-bottom skillet over medium heat. Add the onion and cook, stirring frequently, for 5 minutes, or until softened but not browned.

2 Add the mushrooms, chilies, and garlic and cook, stirring frequently, for 5 minutes, or until the mushrooms are lightly browned. Add the spinach and cook, stirring, for 1–2 minutes, or until just wilted. Add the cheese and stir until just melted.

3 Spoon an equal quantity of the mixture into the center of each tortilla. Fold in the opposite sides of each tortilla to cover the filling, then roll up to enclose it completely.

4 Heat the vegetable oil in a deep-fat fryer or large, deep pan to 350–375°F/180–190°C, or until a cube of bread browns in 30 seconds. Deep-fry the chimichangas 2 at a time, turning once, for 5–6 minutes, or until crisp and golden. Remove with a slotted spoon and drain on paper towels. Keep hot while you cook the remaining chimichangas. Serve with a spoonful of guacamole and sour cream and some chopped tomatoes and onions.

Eggplant and Bean Curry

Look for the Asian eggplants that are very popular in Thai cooking, but if you cannot find them, use the more familiar purple ones.

SERVES 4

PREP TIME 15 MINUTES

COOKING TIME 15 MINUTES

2 tbsp vegetable or peanut oil

1 onion, chopped

2 garlic cloves, crushed

2 fresh red chilies, seeded and chopped

1 tbsp red Thai curry paste

1 large eggplant, cut into chunks

4 oz/115 g Asian or baby eggplants

1 cup shelled baby fava beans

¾ cup fine green beans

1¼ cups vegetable stock

2 oz/55 g creamed coconut, chopped

3 tbsp Thai soy sauce

1 tsp palm sugar or brown sugar

3 kaffir lime leaves, coarsely torn

4 tbsp chopped fresh cilantro

1 Heat the oil in a preheated wok or large skillet over high heat. Add the onion, garlic, and chilies and stir-fry for 1–2 minutes. Add the curry paste and stir-fry for 1–2 minutes.

2 Add the eggplants and cook for 3–4 minutes, or until starting to soften. (You may need to add a little more oil, as eggplants soak it up quickly.) Add all the beans and stir-fry for 2 minutes.

3 Pour in the stock and add the creamed coconut, soy sauce, sugar, and lime leaves. Bring gently to a boil and cook until the coconut has dissolved. Stir in the cilantro and serve immediately.

Cauliflower Cheese

This British favorite is nutritious, suitable for vegetarians, and quite inexpensive. The type and amount of cheese is a matter of personal choice. A mixture of broccoli and cauliflower can be used to give a variation of flavors and textures.

SERVES 4

PREP TIME 15 MINUTES

COOKING TIME 20 MINUTES

1 cauliflower, trimmed and cut into florets (1 lb 8 oz/675 g prepared weight)

3 tbsp butter

5 tbsp all-purpose flour

scant 2 cups milk

generous 1 cup finely grated Cheddar cheese

whole nutmeg, for grating

1 tbsp freshly grated Parmesan cheese

salt and pepper

to serve (optional)

sliced tomatoes

green salad

crusty bread

1 Cook the cauliflower in a pan of boiling salted water for 4–5 minutes —it should still be firm. Drain, then put in a preheated 1½-quart gratin dish and keep warm.

2 Melt the butter in the rinsed-out pan over medium heat and stir in the flour. Cook for 1 minute, stirring constantly.

3 Remove from the heat and gradually stir in the milk until you have a smooth consistency.

4 Return to low heat and continue to stir while the sauce comes to a boil and thickens. Reduce the heat and simmer gently, stirring constantly, for 3 minutes, or until the sauce is creamy and smooth.

5 Remove from the heat and stir in the Cheddar cheese and a good grating of the nutmeg. Taste and season well with salt and pepper.

6 Preheat the broiler to high. Pour the hot sauce over the cauliflower, then top with the Parmesan cheese and cook under the broiler until well browned. Serve immediately with sliced tomatoes, green salad, and some crusty bread, if liked.

Cold Tofu with Chili and Scallion

Tofu is rich in protein and often comes in block form. In this Japanese dish, the block shape is preserved and adds to the overall effect of the beautiful presentation.

SERVES 2

PREP TIME 10 MINUTES

COOKING TIME 5 MINUTES

10½ oz/300 g silken tofu, drained

4 tbsp vegetable oil

2 scallions, thinly sliced

½ fresh red chili, thinly sliced

1 tbsp shoyu (Japanese soy sauce)

1 tsp sesame oil

1 Put the tofu on a heatproof plate and cut the block into cubes, but keep the block intact.

2 Heat the vegetable oil in a small pan over high heat. When hot, add the scallions and chili and wait until they begin to sizzle.

3 Pour the hot oil mixture over the tofu, then sprinkle with the shoyu and sesame oil. Serve as a block.

Chef's tip

Make sure you use silken tofu for this recipe—firm tofu won't give you the right kind of texture combination.

Vegetable Couscous

Couscous is a semolina grain that is widely eaten in North Africa. It is very quick and easy to cook, and makes a pleasant change from rice or pasta. It can also be cooked with milk to make a porridge, or mixed with fruit and served as a dessert.

SERVES 4

PREP TIME 20 MINUTES

COOKING TIME 40 MINUTES

2 tbsp vegetable oil

1 large onion, coarsely chopped

1 carrot, chopped

1 turnip, chopped

2½ cups vegetable stock

1 scant cup couscous

2 tomatoes, peeled and cut into quarters

2 zucchini, chopped

1 red bell pepper, seeded and chopped

scant 1 cup green beans, chopped

grated rind of 1 lemon

pinch of ground turmeric (optional)

1 tbsp finely chopped fresh cilantro or parsley

salt and pepper

fresh flat-leaf parsley sprigs, to garnish

1 Heat the oil in a large pan over medium heat. Add the onion, carrot, and turnip and cook, stirring frequently, for 3–4 minutes. Add the stock and bring to a boil. Reduce the heat, then cover and simmer for 20 minutes.

2 Meanwhile, put the couscous in a heatproof bowl and moisten with a little boiling water. Stir until the grains have swollen and separated.

3 Add the tomatoes, zucchini, red bell pepper, and green beans to the pan and stir.

4 Stir the lemon rind into the couscous, then add the turmeric, if using, and mix thoroughly. Put the couscous in a steamer or a cheesecloth-lined strainer and set it over the pan of vegetables. Simmer the vegetables so that the couscous steams for 8–10 minutes.

5 Season the couscous to taste with salt and pepper, then pile onto warmed serving plates. Ladle the vegetables and some of the liquid over the top. Scatter over the cilantro and serve immediately, garnished with parsley sprigs.

Moorish Zucchini Salad

The combination of toasted pine nuts and raisins has featured in Spanish recipes since the Moors ruled the Iberian Peninsula from AD 711 to 1492. This chilled salad can be spooned onto bread slices as tapas, or served as a first course on lettuce leaves or to accompany a roast chicken buffet.

SERVES 4–6

PREP TIME 10 MINUTES, PLUS 4 HOURS'
COOLING AND CHILLING

COOKING TIME 10 MINUTES

about 4 tbsp olive oil

1 large garlic clove, halved

1 lb 2 oz/500 g small zucchini, thinly sliced
(see Chef's Tip)

generous ⅓ cup pine nuts

⅓ cup raisins

3 tbsp finely chopped mint leaves (not spearmint
or peppermint), plus extra sprigs to garnish

about 2 tbsp lemon juice, or to taste

salt and pepper

1 Heat the oil in a large skillet over medium heat. Add the garlic and let cook until golden to flavor the oil, then remove and discard. Add the zucchini and cook, stirring, until just tender. Immediately remove and transfer to a large serving bowl.

2 Add the pine nuts, raisins, mint, lemon juice, and salt and pepper to taste and stir. Taste and add more oil, lemon juice and seasoning, if necessary.

3 Set aside and let cool completely. Cover and chill in the refrigerator for at least 3½ hours. Remove 10 minutes before serving. Serve garnished with mint sprigs.

Chef's tip

This salad is best made with young, tender zucchini no more than 1 inch/2.5 cm thick. If using older, larger zucchini, cut them in half or quarters lengthwise first, then slice thinly.

Salade Niçoise

Ask ten French chefs for a salade niçoise recipe, and you'll get ten different versions. It is a matter of debate in culinary circles whether this Mediterranean salad should contain tomatoes, green beans, or hard-cooked eggs, but most renditions contain all these ingredients.

SERVES 4–6 AS A MAIN COURSE
PREP TIME 15 MINUTES
COOKING TIME ABOUT 10 MINUTES

2 tuna steaks, about ¾ inch/2 cm thick
olive oil, for brushing
1¾ cups green beans
2 lettuce hearts, leaves separated
3 large hard-cooked eggs, cut into quarters
2 juicy vine-ripened tomatoes, cut into wedges
1¾ oz/50 g anchovy fillets in oil, drained
salt and pepper

dressing
½ cup extra virgin olive oil
3 tbsp white wine vinegar or lemon juice
1–2 garlic cloves, crushed, to taste
1 tsp Dijon mustard
½ tsp superfine sugar

garnishes
generous ⅓ cup Niçoise olives
torn fresh basil leaves

French bread, to serve

1 Preheat a ridged grill pan over high heat. Brush the tuna steaks with oil. Add to the hot grill pan, oiled-side down, and cook for 2 minutes.

2 Lightly brush the top side of the tuna steaks with a little more oil. Use a pair of tongs to turn the tuna steaks over, then season to taste with salt and pepper. Cook for an additional 2 minutes for rare or up to 4 minutes for well-done. Remove and let cool.

3 Meanwhile, bring a pan of salted water to a boil. Add the beans and return to a boil, then boil for 3 minutes, or until tender-crisp. Put all the ingredients for the dressing into a screw-top jar, then screw on the lid and shake vigorously until an emulsion forms. Drain the beans and immediately transfer to a large bowl. Pour over the dressing and stir well. Let the beans cool in the dressing.

4 To serve, line a platter with lettuce leaves. Remove the beans from the dressing, reserving the excess dressing in the bowl, and pile them in the center of the platter. Break the tuna into large flakes and arrange over the beans.

5 Arrange the egg quarters and tomatoes around the side of the platter. Arrange the anchovy fillets over the salad, then scatter with the olives and basil. Drizzle the reserved dressing over everything and serve with plenty of French bread for mopping up the dressing.

Traditional Greek Salad

This is the ubiquitous salad of Greece. Recipes vary enormously and in fact the Greeks use whatever they have to hand. Any kind of salad greens will do, but whichever lettuce you choose, it should be sliced rather than separated into leaves.

SERVES 4

PREP TIME 15 MINUTES

COOKING TIME NO COOKING

dressing

6 tbsp extra virgin olive oil

2 tbsp freshly squeezed lemon juice

1 garlic clove, crushed

pinch of sugar

salt and pepper

7 oz/200 g authentic Greek feta cheese (drained weight)

½ head iceberg lettuce or 1 lettuce, such as romaine or escarole, shredded or sliced

4 tomatoes, cut into quarters

½ cucumber, sliced

12 Greek black olives

2 tbsp chopped fresh herbs such as oregano, flat-leaf parsley, mint, or basil

1 For the dressing, put the oil, lemon juice, garlic, sugar, and salt and pepper to taste in a small bowl and whisk together. Set aside.

2 Cut the feta cheese into 1-inch/2.5-cm cubes. Put the lettuce, tomatoes, and cucumber in a salad bowl. Scatter over the cheese and toss together.

3 Just before serving, whisk the dressing again, then pour over the salad and toss to coat. Scatter over the olives and the chopped herbs and serve immediately.

Tabbouleh

This Middle Eastern salad is becoming increasingly fashionable in other parts of the world. It is a classic accompaniment to lamb, but it also goes well with most grilled or broiled meats. Alternatively, serve it with hummus and pita bread for a vegetarian lunch.

SERVES 4

PREP TIME 10 MINUTES, PLUS 1½ HOURS' STANDING AND MARINATING

COOKING TIME NO COOKING

scant 1 cup bulgar wheat

3 tbsp extra virgin olive oil

4 tbsp lemon juice

4 scallions

1 green bell pepper, seeded and sliced

4 tomatoes, chopped

2 tbsp chopped fresh parsley

2 tbsp chopped fresh mint

8 black olives, pitted

salt and pepper

1 Put the bulgar wheat in a large bowl and add enough cold water to cover. Let stand for 30 minutes, or until the bulgar wheat has doubled in size. Drain well and press out as much liquid as possible. Spread the bulgar wheat out on paper towels to dry.

2 Put the bulgar wheat in a serving bowl. Mix the oil and lemon juice together in a pitcher and season to taste with salt and pepper. Pour the mixture over the bulgar wheat, then cover and let marinate at room temperature for 1 hour.

3 Using a sharp knife, finely chop the scallions, then add to the salad with the green bell pepper, tomatoes, parsley, and chopped mint and toss lightly to mix. Scatter over the olives and serve immediately.

Chef's tip

The bulgar wheat grains have been cracked by boiling and so are already partially cooked; it just needs to be rehydrated. Don't make this salad too far in advance, as it may go soggy.

Hot-and-Sour Noodle and Mushroom Salad

Chili sauces vary in strength, so add the sauce to this Thai-style salad's dressing a little at a time.

SERVES 4

PREP TIME 10 MINUTES, PLUS 5 MINUTES' SOAKING

COOKING TIME NO COOKING

9 oz/250 g rice vermicelli noodles

2 tbsp sesame oil

6 scallions

3 cups white mushrooms

½ cucumber

mixed salad greens, to serve (optional)

dressing

4 tbsp sesame oil

2 tbsp Thai fish sauce

juice of 2 limes

1 tsp sugar

1–2 tsp hot chili sauce

2 tbsp chopped fresh cilantro

1 Soak the noodles in a pan of boiling water according to the package directions until tender. Drain and put in a large bowl. Add the oil and toss until the noodles are well coated.

2 Slice the scallions and mushrooms, then cut the cucumber into short, thin sticks. Add to the noodles in the bowl.

3 For the dressing, put the oil, fish sauce, lime juice, sugar, and chili sauce in a small bowl and whisk together. Stir in the cilantro.

4 Pour the dressing over the salad and toss until well coated. Serve the salad immediately, with some mixed salad greens, if liked.

Mexican Chili Beans

Known as frijoles in Mexico, this dish is traditionally made with black kidney beans, but other types of bean may also be used.

SERVES 4

PREP TIME 15 MINUTES, PLUS 3–4 HOURS' SOAKING

COOKING TIME 2–2¼ HOURS

2 cups dried black kidney or red kidney beans, soaked in cold water for 3–4 hours

1 bay leaf

2 onions, chopped

2 garlic cloves, finely chopped

2–3 fresh green chilies

2 tbsp corn oil

3 tomatoes, peeled, seeded, and chopped

salt and pepper

to serve (optional)

grated mozzarella cheese

baby tomatoes

scallions

flour tortillas

1 Drain the beans, then rinse well and put in a large, heavy-bottom pan. Cover the beans with cold water, then add the bay leaf, half the onions, half the garlic, and the chilies. Bring to a boil and boil rapidly for 15 minutes, skimming off any foam that rises to the surface. Reduce the heat, then cover and simmer for 1 hour, adding more boiling water, if necessary. Add half the oil and simmer for 30–45 minutes, or until tender. Season to taste with salt and set aside.

2 Heat the remaining oil in a skillet over medium heat. Add the remaining onion and garlic and cook, stirring frequently, for 5 minutes, or until softened. Add the tomatoes and cook for an additional 5 minutes.

3 Add 3 tablespoons of the cooked beans to the skillet and mash the mixture thoroughly. Stir the mixture into the remaining beans and reheat gently. Taste and adjust the seasoning, if necessary. Serve with grated mozzarella cheese, baby tomatoes, scallions, and flour tortillas, if liked.

Madras Potatoes

Madras potatoes...Bombay potatoes...similar potato recipes to this appear on most Indian restaurant menus under a variety of names. Waxy potatoes are the best to use because they hold their shape during the rapid frying.

SERVES 4–6

PREP TIME 15 MINUTES, PLUS 30 MINUTES' COOLING

COOKING TIME 15–18 MINUTES

2 lb/900 g new potatoes, scrubbed and halved or cut into quarters

3 tbsp ghee or 3 tbsp vegetable or peanut oil

2 tsp black mustard seeds

1 onion, sliced

4 garlic cloves, very finely chopped

1-inch/2.5-cm piece fresh gingerroot, very finely chopped

1 fresh red chili, seeded or not (to taste), and finely chopped

1 tsp ground cumin

½ tsp ground coriander

salt

chopped fresh cilantro, to garnish

lemon wedges, to serve

1 Put the potatoes in a large pan of salted boiling water over high heat and bring to a boil, then boil for 5–8 minutes, or until tender when pierced with the point of a knife. Drain well, then set aside to cool.

2 Melt the ghee in a kadhai, wok, or large skillet over medium-high heat. Add the mustard seeds and cook, stirring, for 1 minute, or until they start to crackle and jump.

3 Mix in the onion and cook, stirring frequently, for 5 minutes, then stir in the garlic, ginger, and chili and cook until the onion is golden.

4 Add the cumin and ground coriander and stir until well blended. Add the potatoes and cook, stirring, until they are hot and coated with the spices. Add extra salt, if necessary. Sprinkle with the fresh cilantro and serve with lemon wedges.

Chef's tip

Served at room temperature, these make a good chaat, or snack, to serve with an ice-cold beer. Just serve with toothpicks for picking up.

Middle Eastern-Style Zucchini

In this recipe strips of zucchini are combined with pine nuts, anchovies, and garlic to produce a dish bursting with the aromatic flavors of the Middle East.

SERVES 4–6

PREP TIME 15 MINUTES
COOKING TIME 20 MINUTES

1 lb 2 oz/500 g zucchini
3 tbsp olive oil
1 large garlic clove, finely chopped
3 tbsp red or white wine vinegar
3 tbsp water
6–8 anchovy fillets, canned in oil or salted
3 tbsp pine nuts
scant ¼ cup raisins
salt and pepper
fresh flat-leaf parsley sprigs, to garnish

1 Trim the zucchini, then use a sharp knife to cut them into long, thin strips. Heat the oil in a large skillet over medium heat. Add the garlic and cook, stirring, for 2 minutes.

2 Add the zucchini and cook, stirring, until just beginning to turn brown. Add the vinegar and water, then cover and simmer for 10 minutes, stirring occasionally.

3 Meanwhile, drain the anchovies if canned, or rinse well if they are salted. Coarsely chop, then use the back of a wooden spoon to mash them to a paste.

4 Stir the anchovies, pine nuts, and raisins into the skillet. Increase the heat and cook, stirring, until the zucchini are bathed in a thin sauce and are tender. Adjust the seasoning, if necessary, remembering that the anchovies are very salty.

5 Either serve immediately or let cool completely and serve at room temperature. To serve, garnish with parsley sprigs.

Spinach and Ricotta Gnocchi

These mouthwatering Italian dumplings, made with spinach and ricotta cheese, are best served simply, coated in a herb butter and sprinkled with Parmesan cheese.

SERVES 4

PREP TIME 25 MINUTES, PLUS 1½ HOURS' COOLING AND CHILLING

COOKING TIME ABOUT 15 MINUTES

2 lb 4 oz/1 kg fresh spinach, tough stems removed

1½ cups ricotta cheese

1 cup freshly grated Parmesan cheese

3 eggs, lightly beaten

pinch of freshly grated nutmeg

generous ⅔ cup–generous 1 cup all-purpose flour, plus extra for dusting

salt and pepper

herb butter

1 stick unsalted butter

2 tbsp chopped fresh oregano

2 tbsp chopped fresh sage

1 Wash the spinach, then place it in a pan with just the water that clings to its leaves. Cover and cook over low heat for 6–8 minutes, or until just wilted. Drain well and set aside to cool.

2 Squeeze or press out as much liquid as possible from the spinach, then chop finely or process in a food processor or blender. Put the spinach in a bowl and add the ricotta cheese, half the Parmesan cheese, the eggs, and nutmeg and season to taste with salt and pepper. Beat until thoroughly combined. Sift in the flour and lightly work it into the mixture, adding more, if necessary, to make a workable mixture. Cover with plastic wrap and chill in the refrigerator for 1 hour.

3 With floured hands, break off small pieces of the mixture and roll into walnut-size balls. Handle as little as possible, as they are quite delicate. Lightly dust the gnocchi with flour.

4 Bring a large pan of lightly salted water to a boil. Add the gnocchi and cook for 2–3 minutes, or until they rise to the surface. Remove with a slotted spoon, then drain well and set aside.

5 Meanwhile, melt the butter for the herb butter in a large, heavy-bottom skillet over low heat. Add the oregano and sage and cook, stirring, for 1 minute. Add the gnocchi and toss gently for 1 minute to coat. Transfer to a warmed serving dish, then sprinkle with the remaining Parmesan cheese and serve immediately.

Perfect Creamed Potato

Creamed potato is one of Britain's most long-standing comfort foods, but it has to be smooth and creamy, not lumpy. Using the right potato is essential—you need mealy potatoes such as Yukon or a good all-rounder like Russet—and hot milk creates a creamier result.

SERVES 4

PREP TIME 10 MINUTES

COOKING TIME 25–30 MINUTES

2 lb/900 g floury potatoes, such as Russet or Yukon

4 tbsp salted/unsalted butter

3 tbsp hot milk

salt and pepper

1 Peel the potatoes, putting them in cold water as you prepare the others to prevent discoloration.

2 Bring a large pan of water to a boil. Cut the potatoes into even-size chunks, then add to the pan and cook over medium heat, covered, for 20–25 minutes, or until tender. Test with the point of a knife, but do make sure you test right to the middle to avoid lumps.

3 Remove from the heat and drain. Return the potatoes to the hot pan and mash with a potato masher until smooth.

4 Add the butter and continue to mash until incorporated, then add the milk.

5 Taste the mash and season to taste with salt and pepper, as necessary. Serve immediately.

Desserts

Here is a collection of irresistible desserts to delight every palate, whatever the occasion.

Asian-Style Grilled Bananas

Grilled bananas are beautifully sweet, yet healthy to eat. This Asian recipe contrasts their sweetness with the tartness of lime and an indulgence of heavy cream.

SERVES 4

PREP TIME 10 MINUTES, PLUS 10 MINUTES' COOLING

COOKING TIME 8 MINUTES

2 oz/55 g creamed coconut, chopped

⅔ cup heavy cream

4 bananas

juice and rind of 1 lime, plus 2 limes, cut into wedges

1 tbsp vegetable or peanut oil

½ cup dry unsweetened coconut

1 Put the creamed coconut and cream in a small pan over low heat and heat gently until the coconut has dissolved. Remove from the heat and set aside to cool for 10 minutes. Whisk until thick but floppy.

2 Preheat a ridged grill pan over high heat. Peel the bananas, cut them into thirds, and toss them in the lime juice and rind in a bowl. Lightly brush the hot grill pan with the oil, then add the bananas and cook, turning once, for 2–3 minutes, or until softened and browned. Just before the end of the cooking time, add the lime wedges to the pan and heat through.

3 Meanwhile, preheat the broiler to high. Toast the dry unsweetened coconut on a piece of foil under the broiler until lightly browned. Serve the bananas with the lime wedges and coconut cream, sprinkled with the toasted coconut.

Winter Rice Pudding with Dried Fruits

In China this richly exotic dish is traditionally eaten on the eighth day of the twelfth month of the lunar calendar. Versions of rice pudding are eaten all over the world, and it is often highly prized as a comfort food.

Serves 6–8

Prep Time 10 minutes, plus 2 hours' soaking

Cooking Time 1 hour 10 minutes

generous 1 cup glutinous rice

1 tbsp peanuts

1 tbsp pine nuts

1 tbsp lotus seeds

8 oz/225 g mixed dried fruits (raisins, kumquats, prunes, dates, etc.)

8 cups water

generous ½ cup sugar

1 Soak the rice in a bowl of cold water for at least 2 hours, then drain well. Meanwhile, soak the peanuts, pine nuts, and lotus seeds in a separate bowl of cold water for at least 1 hour, then drain well. Soak the dried fruits as necessary, then drain well. Chop all the larger fruits into small pieces.

2 Bring the water to a boil in a pan, then add the sugar and stir until dissolved. Add the drained rice, peanuts, pine nuts, lotus seeds, and dried fruits. Return to a boil, then reduce the heat to very low and gently simmer, covered, for 1 hour, stirring frequently.

Chef's tip

The texture of this dish should be that of a very thick soup. Simply add more water to create a slightly thinner version.

Mousse au Chocolat

As the perfect make-ahead dessert for a bistro-style meal, this rich, elegant mousse, laced with French brandy or liqueur, will not disappoint.

SERVES 4–6

PREP TIME 15 MINUTES, PLUS 3 HOURS' CHILLING

COOKING TIME 5 MINUTES

8 squares semisweet chocolate, chopped

2 tbsp brandy, Grand Marnier, or Cointreau

4 tbsp water

¼ stick unsalted butter, diced

3 large eggs, separated

¼ tsp cream of tartar

4 tbsp superfine sugar

½ cup heavy cream

1 Put the chocolate, brandy, and water in a small pan over low heat and heat, stirring, until the chocolate has melted and is smooth. Remove from the heat and beat in the butter.

2 Beat the egg yolks into the chocolate mixture, one at a time, until blended, then let cool slightly.

3 Meanwhile, using an electric mixer on low speed, beat the egg whites in a spotlessly clean bowl until frothy, then gradually increase the mixer's speed and beat until soft peaks form. Sprinkle the cream of tartar over the surface, then add the sugar, tablespoon by tablespoon, and continue beating until stiff peaks form. Beat several tablespoons of the egg whites into the chocolate mixture to loosen.

4 In a separate bowl, whip the cream until soft peaks form. Spoon the cream over the chocolate mixture, then spoon the remaining egg whites over the cream. Fold the chocolate mixture into the cream and egg whites with a large metal spoon or rubber spatula.

5 Either spoon the chocolate mousse into a large serving bowl or divide between 4 or 6 individual bowls. Cover the bowl(s) with plastic wrap and chill in the refrigerator for at least 3 hours before serving.

Caution

Recipes using raw eggs should be avoided by infants, the elderly, pregnant women, convalescents, and anyone suffering from an illness.

Peach and Pecan Empanadas

These sweet Tex-Mex-style empanadas have a creamy, fruity filling and a hint of crunchy nut. Serve as a sweet snack or a dessert.

MAKES 8

PREP TIME 20 MINUTES

COOKING TIME 20 MINUTES

12 oz/350 g ready-made puff pastry, thawed if frozen

all-purpose flour, for dusting

3 fresh ripe peaches

⅔ cup sour cream

4 tbsp soft light brown sugar

4 tbsp pecan halves, toasted and finely chopped

beaten egg, for sealing and glazing

superfine sugar, for sprinkling

1 Preheat the oven to 400°F/200°C. Roll out the pastry on a lightly floured counter. Using a 6-inch/15-cm saucer as a guide, cut out 8 circles.

2 Cut a small cross in the stem end of each peach. Lower into a pan of boiling water and let stand for 30 seconds. Drain and cool under cold running water. Peel with a small knife, then slice.

3 Put a spoonful of sour cream in the center of each pastry circle and top with a few peach slices. Sprinkle over a little brown sugar and some nuts. Brush each edge with a little beaten egg, then fold the pastry over the filling and press the edges together to seal. Crimp the edges with a fork and prick the tops.

4 Put on a baking sheet, then brush with beaten egg to glaze and sprinkle with superfine sugar. Bake in the oven for 20 minutes, or until golden brown. Serve warm.

Lemon Meringue Pie

This classic American pie has been a great favorite since the 1960s, when it was available in many restaurants. It has three distinct parts: the crisp pastry base; the tangy, smooth lemon center; and the meringue topping, crispy on the outside yet oozing and marshmallowy inside.

SERVES 8–10

PREP TIME 30 MINUTES, PLUS 40 MINUTES' CHILLING AND COOLING

COOKING TIME 50 MINUTES–1 HOUR

salted/unsalted butter, for greasing

9 oz/250 g ready-made unsweetened pie dough, thawed if frozen

all-purpose flour, for dusting

3 tbsp cornstarch

scant ½ cup superfine sugar

grated rind of 3 lemons

1¼ cups cold water

⅔ cup lemon juice

3 egg yolks

½ stick unsalted butter, diced

meringue

3 egg whites

scant 1 cup superfine sugar

1 tsp golden granulated sugar

1 Grease a 10-inch/25-cm fluted flan pan with butter. Roll out the pastry on a lightly floured counter into a circle 2 inches/5 cm larger than the flan pan. Ease the pastry into the pan without stretching and press down lightly into the corners and trim the edge. Prick the base with a fork and chill, uncovered, in the refrigerator for 20–30 minutes.

2 Preheat the oven to 400°F/200°C. Line the pastry shell with parchment paper and fill with dried beans. Bake on a preheated baking sheet for 15 minutes. Remove the beans and paper and return to the oven for 10 minutes, or until the pastry is dry and just colored. Remove from the oven and reduce the temperature to 300°F/150°C.

3 Put the cornstarch, superfine sugar, and lemon rind in a pan. Pour in a little of the water and blend to a smooth paste. Gradually add the remaining water and the lemon juice. Bring the mixture to a boil over medium heat, stirring constantly. Simmer gently for 1 minute, or until smooth and glossy. Remove from the heat and beat in the egg yolks, one at a time, then beat in the butter. Put the pan in a bowl of cold water to cool the filling. When cool, spoon into the pastry shell.

4 For the meringue, whisk the egg whites with an electric mixer until soft peaks form. Add the superfine sugar gradually, whisking well with each addition, until glossy and firm. Spoon over the filling to cover it completely. Swirl the meringue into peaks and sprinkle with the golden sugar. Bake for 20–30 minutes, or until the meringue is crispy and pale gold but still soft in the center. Let cool slightly before serving.

# Baklava

This melt-in-the-mouth dish is a traditional Middle Eastern dessert. It is made with phyllo pastry, chopped nuts, and sweet spices, drizzled with melted butter and honey.

SERVES 4

PREP TIME 20 MINUTES

COOKING TIME 1 HOUR

scant 1½ cups shelled pistachios, finely chopped

½ cup toasted hazelnuts, finely chopped

½ cup blanched hazelnuts, finely chopped

grated rind of 1 lemon

1 tbsp soft light brown sugar

1 tsp ground pumpkin pie spice

1⅜ sticks salted/unsalted butter, melted, plus extra for greasing

9 oz/250 g (about 16 sheets) frozen phyllo pastry, thawed

1 cup water

2 tbsp honey

1 tbsp lemon juice

1½ cups superfine sugar

½ tsp ground cinnamon

1 Preheat the oven to 325°F/160°C. Put all the nuts, lemon rind, brown sugar, and pumpkin pie spice in a bowl and mix well.

2 Grease a round cake pan, 7 inches/18 cm in diameter and 2 inches/ 5 cm deep, with butter. Cut the whole stack of phyllo sheets to the size of the pan. Keep the phyllo circles covered with a damp dish towel. Lay one circle on the base of the pan and brush with melted butter.

3 Add another 6 circles on top, brushing between each layer with melted butter. Spread over one-third of the nut mixture, then add 3 circles of buttered phyllo. Spread over another third of the nut mixture, then top with 3 more circles of buttered phyllo.

4 Spread over the remaining nut mixture and add the last 3 circles of buttered phyllo. Cut into wedges, then bake in the oven for 1 hour.

5 Meanwhile, put the water, honey, lemon juice, superfine sugar, and cinnamon into a pan. Bring to a boil, stirring constantly. Reduce the heat and simmer, without stirring, for 15 minutes. Let cool. Remove the baklava from the oven, pour over the syrup and let set before serving.

Mexican Chocolate Crème Caramel

This silken dessert with its caramel topping is traditional in Mexico and is commonly known as "flan." The addition of chocolate makes it even more luxurious and tempting.

SERVES 4

PREP TIME 15 MINUTES, PLUS 2 HOURS' COOLING AND CHILLING

COOKING TIME 1¼ HOURS

generous ½ cup granulated sugar

4 tbsp water

2½ cups milk

2 squares semisweet chocolate, grated

4 eggs

2 tbsp superfine sugar

1 tsp vanilla extract

blueberries and raspberries, to decorate

1 Preheat the oven to 325°F/160°C. Put a 4-cup soufflé dish in the oven to heat.

2 Put the granulated sugar and water in a heavy-bottom pan over low heat. Heat, stirring, until the sugar has dissolved. Bring to a boil, without stirring, and boil until caramelized. Pour into the hot dish, tipping it to coat the base and side. Let cool.

3 Put the milk and chocolate in a separate pan over low heat and heat, stirring occasionally, until the chocolate has dissolved.

4 Meanwhile, beat the eggs and superfine sugar together in a bowl with a wooden spoon. Gradually beat in the chocolate milk. Add the vanilla extract, then pour into the prepared dish.

5 Stand the dish in a roasting pan and fill the pan with enough lukewarm water to come halfway up the side of the dish. Bake in the oven for 1 hour, or until set. Let cool, then invert onto a serving plate. Chill in the refrigerator before serving, decorated with berries.

Creamy Mango Brûlée

Here a tropical twist is given to a traditional French dish. This is a beautifully indulgent yet light dessert, made with creamy mascarpone cheese and the succulent flesh of mangoes. It makes a perfect finish for any meal.

SERVES 4

PREP TIME 15 MINUTES, PLUS 4 HOURS' CHILLING AND COOLING

COOKING TIME 2–3 MINUTES

2 ripe mangoes

1⅛ cups mascarpone cheese

generous ¾ cup strained plain yogurt

1 tsp ground ginger

grated rind and juice of 1 lime

2 tbsp soft light brown sugar

8 tbsp raw brown sugar

1 Slice each mango lengthwise on either side of the flat central seed. Peel the mango pieces and chop the flesh. Slice off any remaining flesh around the seed, then chop. Divide the mango between 4 ramekins.

2 Beat the mascarpone cheese with the yogurt in a bowl. Fold in the ginger, lime rind and juice, and brown sugar. Divide the mixture between the ramekins and level off the tops. Cover with plastic wrap and chill in the refrigerator for 2 hours.

3 Preheat the broiler to high. Sprinkle 2 tablespoons of the raw brown sugar over the top of each dish, covering the creamy mixture. Cook under the broiler for 2–3 minutes, or until the topping is melted and browned. Let cool, then chill in the refrigerator until ready to serve. This dessert should be eaten on the day of making.

Carrot Halva

This is an example of the very sweet desserts most Indians adore. Originally from the Punjab and northern India, this rich, filling dessert can be served hot or chilled. In winter, it is served hot with ice cream.

SERVES 4–6

PREP TIME 15 MINUTES

COOKING TIME 2¾ HOURS

3 cups milk

⅔ cup light cream

1 lb 2 oz/500 g carrots, coarsely grated

scant ½ cup superfine sugar

1 tbsp soft dark brown sugar

4 tbsp ghee or salted/unsalted butter, melted

1 cup ground almonds

seeds of 6 green cardamom pods, lightly crushed

3 tbsp raisins or golden raisins

to decorate

chopped toasted blanched almonds and pistachios

silver leaf (optional)

1 Rinse a large, heavy-bottom pan with cold water and do not dry. Pour the milk and cream into the pan, then stir in the carrots and heat over medium heat. Slowly bring to a boil, stirring.

2 Reduce the heat to its lowest setting and simmer, stirring frequently, for 2 hours, or until most of the milk has evaporated and the carrots have thickened.

3 Stir in the sugars. Simmer for an additional 30 minutes, stirring constantly to prevent the mixture catching on the bottom of the pan.

4 Stir in the ghee, ground almonds, cardamom seeds, and raisins. Simmer, stirring constantly, until the mixture is thick and there is a thin layer of ghee on the surface.

5 Stir the pudding well, then transfer to a serving dish. Sprinkle the surface with the chopped nuts and add thin flecks of silver leaf, if liked (see Chef's Tip).

Chef's tip

For a special occasion, the top of this dish is traditionally decorated with thin edible silver, called silver leaf or varak. It is sold in upmarket Indian food stores, and each sheet of silver leaf has a paper backing. Put the silver side down onto the pudding and use a paintbrush or pastry brush to dab onto the paper backing to transfer the silver to the pudding. Do not touch the silver with your fingers, or it will stick.

"Jeweled" Honey Mousses

This dessert originated in southern Spain, and has a distinctly Moorish influence. The pomegranate seeds give the beautiful "jeweled" effect and a distinctive tart-sweet flavor.

SERVES 6

PREP TIME 15 MINUTES, PLUS 8 HOURS' FREEZING

COOKING TIME NO COOKING

1 large egg, plus 3 large egg yolks

½ cup honey

1¼ cups heavy cream

3 pomegranates, to serve

1 Line 6 ramekins with pieces of plastic wrap large enough to extend over the tops and set aside.

2 Put the whole egg, egg yolks, and honey in a large bowl and beat until blended and fluffy. Put the cream in a separate bowl and beat until stiff peaks form. Fold the cream into the egg-and-honey mixture.

3 Divide the mixture between the ramekins, then fold the excess plastic wrap over the top of each. Put in the freezer for at least 8 hours until firm. These mousses can be served directly from the freezer, because the texture isn't solid.

4 To serve, unfold the plastic wrap, then invert each ramekin onto a serving plate and remove the ramekin and plastic wrap. Cut the pomegranates in half and hold one half over each mousse in turn. Use your other hand to tap firmly on the base of the pomegranate, so that the seeds fall over the mousse. Serve immediately.

Caution

Recipes using raw eggs should be avoided by infants, the elderly, pregnant women, convalescents, and anyone suffering from an illness.

Apple Pancakes with Maple Syrup Butter

These sweetly spiced apple pancakes, bathed in a sumptuous maple syrup butter, are an upmarket take on an all-American everyday favorite.

SERVES 4–6 MAKES 18
PREP TIME 10 MINUTES
COOKING TIME 20 MINUTES

1⅓ cups self-rising flour, sifted
generous ½ cup superfine sugar
1 tsp ground cinnamon
1 egg
generous ¾ cup milk
2 apples, peeled and grated
1 tbsp salted/unsalted butter
strawberries, to serve

maple syrup butter
⅞ stick salted/unsalted butter, softened
3 tbsp maple syrup

1 Mix the flour, sugar, and cinnamon together in a bowl and make a well in the center. Beat the egg and the milk together and pour into the well. Using a wooden spoon, gently incorporate the dry ingredients into the liquid until well combined, then stir in the apple.

2 Heat the butter in a large, nonstick skillet over low heat until melted and bubbling. Add tablespoons of the pancake mixture to form 3½-inch/9-cm circles. Cook each pancake for 1 minute, or until it starts to bubble lightly on the top and looks set, then flip it over and cook the other side for 30 seconds, or until cooked through. The pancakes should be golden brown; if not, increase the heat a little. Remove and keep warm while you cook the remaining pancake batter (it is not necessary to add extra butter).

3 For the maple syrup butter, melt the butter with the maple syrup in a pan over low heat and stir until combined. To serve, place the pancakes on serving dishes and spoon over the flavored butter. Serve warm with some ripe strawberries for added color and flavor.

Chef's tip

As the batter sits, it tends to thicken up and can make the pancakes very doughy. If the mixture becomes too thick while you are cooking the pancakes, add a little extra milk before continuing.

Ricotta Cheesecake

This melt-in-the-mouth cheesecake confirms a widely held belief that all the best Italian desserts come from Sicily.

SERVES 6–8

PREP TIME 25 MINUTES, PLUS 30 MINUTES' CHILLING

COOKING TIME 45–50 MINUTES

pie dough

scant 1¼ cups all-purpose flour, plus extra for dusting

3 tbsp superfine sugar

pinch of salt

1 stick unsalted butter, chilled and diced

1 egg yolk

filling

2 cups ricotta cheese

½ cup heavy cream

2 eggs, plus 1 egg yolk

scant ½ cup superfine sugar

finely grated rind of 1 lemon

finely grated rind of 1 orange

1 For the pie dough, sift the flour with the sugar and salt onto a counter and make a well in the center. Add the butter and egg yolk to the well and, using your fingertips, gradually work in the flour mixture.

2 Gather up the dough and knead lightly. Cut off one-quarter, then wrap in plastic wrap and chill in the refrigerator. Press the remaining dough into the base and up the side of a 9-inch/23-cm loose-bottom flan pan. Chill, uncovered, in the refrigerator for 30 minutes.

3 Meanwhile, preheat the oven to 375°F/190°C. For the filling, beat the ricotta cheese, cream, eggs and egg yolk, sugar, and lemon and orange rinds together in a bowl. Cover with plastic wrap and chill in the refrigerator until required.

4 Prick the bottom of the pastry shell with a fork. Line with parchment paper, and fill with dried beans. Bake in the oven for 15 minutes. Remove the beans and paper; stand the pan on a cooling rack to cool.

5 Spoon the ricotta mixture into the pastry shell and smooth the surface. Roll out the reserved pastry on a lightly floured surface and cut it into strips. Arrange the strips over the filling in a lattice pattern, brushing the overlapping ends with water so that they stick.

6 Bake in the oven for 30–35 minutes, or until the top is golden and the filling has set. Cool on a cooling rack before lifting off the side of the pan. Cut into wedges to serve.

Coconut Ice Cream with Tropical Fruits

If you have a fresh coconut, its grated flesh can be used instead of the dry unsweetened coconut in this wonderful Caribbean dessert. Malibu is a coconut-flavored liqueur, which blends well with the ice cream, but you could use white rum.

SERVES 6

PREP TIME 25 MINUTES, PLUS 2–6 HOURS' COOLING, FREEZING, AND CHILLING

COOKING TIME 15–20 MINUTES

2½ cups coconut milk
generous ¾ cup superfine sugar
6 egg yolks
scant 2 cups dry unsweetened coconut
⅔ cup heavy cream
1 tbsp Malibu (optional)

tropical fruits
2 papayas, peeled and seeded
2 carambola
2 kiwifruit, peeled
1 tbsp superfine sugar
4 tbsp Malibu (optional)

1 Pour the coconut milk into a pan and heat over low heat. Remove from the heat. Put the sugar and egg yolks in a large bowl and whisk together until pale and the mixture leaves a trail when the whisk is lifted. Slowly add the coconut milk, stirring constantly with a wooden spoon. Pour into the rinsed-out pan or a double boiler and cook over low heat for 10–15 minutes, stirring constantly, until the mixture thickens enough to coat the back of the spoon. You may find that the mixture starts to separate, and if it does, simply whisk it vigorously until it is smooth again. Do not let the mixture boil, or it will curdle.

2 Remove from the heat and stir in the coconut, then let cool for at least 1 hour, stirring from time to time to prevent a skin from forming.

3 Meanwhile, whip the cream in a bowl until it just holds its shape. Cover and refrigerate until required. When the custard is cold, add the Malibu, if using, and mix well together.

4 If using an ice-cream machine, fold the custard into the cream, then churn the mixture in the machine following the manufacturer's directions. Alternatively, freeze the custard in a freezerproof container, uncovered, for 1–2 hours, or until it begins to set around the edges. Turn into a bowl and beat with a fork until smooth. Fold in the cream. Freeze for another 2–3 hours, or until firm. Cover with a lid for storing.

5 Thinly slice the fruits and put in a shallow dish with the sugar and Malibu, if using. Cover and chill for 2–3 hours. Serve with the ice cream.

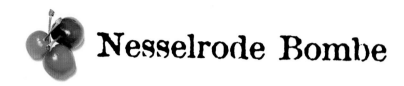

Nesselrode Bombe

Nesselrode is the name given to a selection of dishes, all of which contain chestnut purée. It is named after a 19th-century Russian diplomat, and is an ideal dessert to serve at Christmas.

SERVES 8

PREP TIME 20 MINUTES, PLUS 7 HOURS' STANDING, COOLING, AND FREEZING

COOKING TIME 15–20 MINUTES

6 oz/175 g mixed dried fruits

4 tbsp cherry brandy

1¼ cups light cream

1 vanilla bean

4 egg yolks

scant ½ cup superfine sugar

1¼ cups canned peeled chestnuts

1¼ cups heavy cream

scant ¼ cup candied cherries, chopped

1 Put the dried fruits in a bowl, then add the cherry brandy and stir together. Cover and let soak for 2–3 hours, stirring occasionally, until the liquid is absorbed. Meanwhile, pour the light cream into a heavy-bottom pan, then add the vanilla bean and bring almost to a boil. Remove from the heat and let infuse for 15 minutes.

2 Put the egg yolks and sugar in a large bowl and whisk together until pale and the mixture leaves a trail when the whisk is lifted. Remove the vanilla bean from the cream, then slowly add the cream to the egg mixture, stirring constantly with a wooden spoon.

3 Pour the mixture into the rinsed-out pan or a double boiler and cook over low heat for 10–15 minutes, stirring constantly, until the mixture thickens enough to coat the back of the spoon. Do not let the mixture boil, or it will curdle. Remove the custard from the heat and let cool for at least 1 hour, stirring from time to time to prevent a skin from forming.

4 Put the chestnuts in a food processor or blender and process to form a purée. Whip the heavy cream in a bowl until it just holds its shape. Fold in the soaked fruits and the cherries until well blended.

5 When the custard is cold, add the chestnut purée and whisk together. Fold in the cream and fruit mixture, then pour into a 1½-quart ovenproof bowl. Cover and freeze for at least 5 hours before serving, to enable it to firm.

Japanese Green Tea Sherbet

This is a particularly refreshing sherbet to serve on a hot summer's day or as a dessert to follow a substantial meal. Other suitable teas are Earl Grey and peppermint.

SERVES 6

PREP TIME 15 MINUTES, PLUS 1½–7 HOURS' COOLING AND FREEZING

COOKING TIME 15 MINUTES

3¾ cups water

generous ¾ cup superfine sugar

4 tbsp Japanese green tea leaves

2 tbsp lemon juice

2 egg whites

1 Put 2½ cups of the water in a heavy-bottom pan, then add the sugar and heat gently, stirring, until the sugar has dissolved. Bring to a boil, then reduce the heat and simmer, without stirring, for 10 minutes, to form a syrup. Do not let it brown. Remove from the heat and let cool for at least 1 hour.

2 Meanwhile, bring the remaining water to a boil in a separate pan. Pour over the tea leaves in a heatproof bowl and let infuse for 10 minutes. Strain the tea liquid. When the syrup is cold, add the tea and lemon juice and stir together until well mixed.

3 If using an ice-cream machine, churn the mixture in the machine following the manufacturer's directions. When the mixture begins to freeze, whisk the egg whites until they just hold their shape but are not dry, then fold into the mixture and continue churning. Alternatively, freeze the mixture in a freezerproof container, uncovered, for 3–4 hours, or until mushy. Turn the mixture into a bowl and beat with a fork until smooth. Lightly whisk the egg whites until they just hold their shape but are not dry, then fold them into the mixture. Freeze again for 3–4 hours, or until firm. Cover with a lid for storing. Serve in scoops.

Caution

Recipes using raw eggs should be avoided by infants, the elderly, pregnant women, convalescents, and anyone suffering from an illness.

Guava, Lime, and Tequila Sherbet

When you want to chill out, literally, this ice-cold Mexican-style dessert will hit the spot. Decorate with lime twists or finely pared strips of rind instead of lime wedges for additional elegance.

SERVES 4

PREP TIME 15 MINUTES, PLUS 5½ HOURS' COOLING AND CHILLING

COOKING TIME 10 MINUTES

generous ¾ cup superfine sugar

generous 1¾ cups water

4 fresh ripe guavas or 8 canned guava halves

2 tbsp tequila

juice of ½ lime, or to taste

1 egg white

lime wedges, to decorate

1 Put the sugar and water in a heavy-bottom pan over low heat and heat, stirring, until the sugar has dissolved. When the liquid turns clear, bring to a boil and boil for 5 minutes, without stirring, or until a thick syrup forms. Remove from the heat and let cool.

2 Cut the fresh guavas, if using, in half. Scoop out the flesh. Discard the seeds from the fresh or canned guava flesh. Transfer to a food processor or blender and process until smooth.

3 Add the fruit purée to the syrup with the tequila and lime juice to taste. Transfer the mixture to a freezerproof container and freeze for 1 hour, or until slushy.

4 Remove from the freezer and process again until smooth. Return to the freezer and freeze for 2 hours, or until firm. Process again until smooth. With the motor still running, add the egg white through the feed tube. Freeze for an additional 2 hours, or until firm.

5 Transfer the sherbet to the refrigerator 15 minutes before serving. Serve in scoops, decorated with lime wedges.

Caution

Recipes using raw eggs should be avoided by infants, the elderly, pregnant women, convalescents, and anyone suffering from an illness.

Poached Fruit Seville-Style

The Moorish influence on Spanish cuisine is very evident in Andalusia, with the generous use of fruit and spices. Tender, juicy apricots are used in this recipe, but many other tree fruits, such as pears or nectarines, are also delicious. Serve the fruit on their own or with vanilla ice cream.

SERVES 4–6

PREP TIME 15 MINUTES, PLUS 45 MINUTES'
COOLING AND CHILLING

COOKING TIME 20–25 MINUTES

½ tsp fennel seeds
½ tsp coriander seeds
¼ tsp black peppercorns
1 cup superfine sugar
scant 1 cup red wine, such as Rioja
scant 1 cup water
3 tbsp freshly squeezed orange juice
2 tbsp freshly squeezed lemon juice
2 tbsp Spanish cream sherry
3 cloves
1 cinnamon stick
12 tender apricots, halved and pitted
2 tbsp slivered almonds, toasted, to decorate

1 Put the fennel and coriander seeds and peppercorns in a heavy-bottom pan over high heat and dry-fry for up to 1 minute, or until fragrant. Immediately tip out of the pan to prevent additional cooking. Put in a mortar and lightly crush with a pestle.

2 Put the sugar, wine, water, orange and lemon juices, sherry, and all the spices in a heavy-bottom pan and heat over medium-high heat, stirring, until the sugar has dissolved. Bring to a boil, without stirring, and let bubble for 5 minutes.

3 Add the fruit and simmer for 6–8 minutes, or until tender. Remove the pan from the heat, then transfer the apricots to a bowl of iced water and let cool. When cool enough to handle, remove the apricots and peel. Cover and chill in the refrigerator until required.

4 Meanwhile, return the juices to the heat and boil until the syrup thickens and the flavors become more concentrated. Remove from the heat and let cool.

5 When ready to serve, divide the fruit between serving bowls, then spoon the syrup over and sprinkle with slivered almonds to decorate.

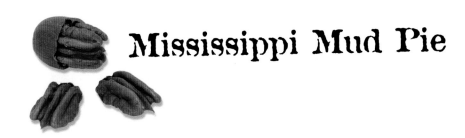

Mississippi Mud Pie

This classic American chilled chocolate pie with pecans from the deep South is extremely appetizing. It is so rich that thin slices will satisfy even the most hearty appetites.

SERVES 12–14

PREP TIME 20 MINUTES, PLUS 30 MINUTES'
COOLING AND CHILLING

COOKING TIME 35 MINUTES

crumb crust

5 oz/140 g graham crackers

generous ½ cup pecans, finely chopped

1 tbsp soft light brown sugar

½ tsp ground cinnamon

¾ stick salted/unsalted butter, melted

filling

2 sticks salted/unsalted butter or margarine, plus extra for greasing

6 squares semisweet chocolate, chopped

½ cup corn syrup

4 large eggs, beaten

generous ½ cup pecans, finely chopped

whipped cream, to serve

1 Preheat the oven to 350°F/180°C. Lightly grease a 9-inch/23-cm springform or loose-bottom flan pan.

2 For the crumb crust, put the graham crackers, pecans, sugar, and cinnamon into a food processor and process until fine crumbs form—do not overprocess to a powder. Add the butter and process again until moistened.

3 Tip the crumb mixture into the flan pan and press over the bottom and about 1½ inches/4 cm up the side of the pan. Cover and chill in the refrigerator while you make the filling.

4 For the filling, put the butter, chocolate, and corn syrup in a pan over low heat and heat, stirring, until melted and blended. Let cool, then beat in the eggs and pecans.

5 Pour the filling into the chilled crumb crust and smooth the surface. Bake in the oven for 30 minutes, or until just set but still soft in the center. Let cool on a cooling rack. Serve at room temperature or chilled, with whipped cream.

Steamed Syrup Sponge Pudding

This is probably Britain's favorite pudding—steamed to give a light, moist sponge just oozing with syrup. Children and adults alike love it.

SERVES 6

PREP TIME 15 MINUTES

COOKING TIME 1½ HOURS

1 stick salted/unsalted butter, plus extra for greasing

2 tbsp corn syrup, plus extra to serve

generous ½ cup superfine sugar

2 eggs, lightly beaten

scant 1½ cups self-rising flour

2 tbsp milk

grated rind of 1 lemon

1 Grease a 5-cup ovenproof bowl with butter and spoon the syrup into the base.

2 Beat the butter and sugar together in a bowl until soft and creamy, then beat in the eggs, a little at a time. Fold in the flour and stir in the milk to make a soft dropping consistency. Add the lemon rind. Turn the mixture into the ovenproof bowl.

3 Cover the surface with a circle of waxed or parchment paper and top with a pleated sheet of foil. Secure with some string or crimp the edges of the foil to ensure a tight fit around the bowl.

4 Put the pudding in a large pan half-filled with boiling water. Cover and return to a boil over medium heat. Reduce the heat to a slow simmer and steam for 1½ hours, or until risen and firm. Keep checking the water level and top off with boiling water as necessary.

5 Heat a little more corn syrup in a pan. Remove the pudding pan from the heat and lift out the ovenproof bowl. Remove the cover and loosen the pudding from the sides of the bowl using a knife. Turn out into a warmed dish and serve with the extra corn syrup.

Index